OUT OF IRELAND

THE STORY OF IRISH EMIGRATION TO AMERICA

By Kerby Miller and Paul Wagner

Roberts Rinehart Publishers

TABLE OF CONTENTS

ACKNOWLEDGMENTS

THIS BOOK HAS ITS GENESIS in the creation of the documentary film, also titled *Out of Ireland*, which first brought the two of us together as collaborators almost five years ago. The film (supported by a grant from the National Endowment for the Humanities) is based on scholarly materials but designed for presentation to a large viewing public. Our work on it left us convinced that the story of the Irish people's trans-Atlantic adventure could similarly be presented in book form. We sincerely hope that we have succeeded in telling their story with the power and compassion it deserves.

In our attempt to create a popularly appealing book, we have taken liberties in the presentation of our primary source of historical evidence—the remarkable memoirs and letters written by and to the Irish immigrants in America. Thus the documents have been extensively edited, and often drastically shortened, in order to focus attention on particular aspects of the immigrants' experiences in the New World and their memories of the Old. We would encourage interested readers to look for the forthcoming volume from Oxford University Press, written by Kerby Miller, Arnold Schrier, Bruce Boling, and David Doyle, which will present the complete, unedited memoirs and letters and provide more extensive and more scholarly interpretations of the material.

All of the letters and memoirs have been selected from Kerby Miller's collection, but we are indebted to the various archives and families that are the original sources of the documents and have granted us permission for their use. They are listed in the credit section at the end of the book.

Because it was the story line and visualization of the documentary film that established the creative direction for the book, we owe a debt of thanks to our many collaborators on the film. They include especially the interviewees in the film whose insights and enthusiasm for the subject have informed and inspired us: Mick Moloney, Hasia Diner, John B. Keane, and Dennis Clark. We want also to recognize the valuable contributions of scholars Charles Fanning, George O'Brien, Arnold Schrier, David Doyle, and Bruce Boling.

For those interested in reading deeper into the subject of Irish emigration to America, we enthusiastically recommend several fine studies by our consultants, including Dennis Clark's *Hibernia America: The Irish and Regional Cultures* (New York: Greenwood Press, 1988); Hasia Diner's *Erin's Daughters in America: Irish Immigrant Women in the Nineteenth Century* (Baltimore: Johns Hopkins Press, 1983); David Doyle's *Ireland, Irishmen, and Revolutionary America, 1760-1820* (Dublin and Cork: Mercier Press, 1981); Charles Fanning's *The Irish Voice in*

America: Irish-American Fiction from the 1760s to the 1980s (Lexington: The University of Kentucky, 1990); Arnold Schrier's *Ireland and the American Emigration, 1850-1900* (New York: Russell & Russell, 1970); and Kerby Miller's *Emigrants and Exiles: Ireland and the Irish Exodus to North America* (New York: Oxford University Press, 1985). John B. Keane and George O'Brien each have published several volumes of fiction that illuminate life in the Irish countryside from which the mass of Irish emigrants have sprung.

Ellen Casey Wagner, the producer of the film (and wife of one of the authors) has been a constant source of good judgment and enthusiastic support as the book has taken form. We are much in her debt.

Our coproducer Dorothy Peterson, historical researcher Beth Ruffin McIntyre, director of photography Erich Roland, location consultant Jack Burtchaell, and editors Neil Means and Reid Oechslin all made contributions to the film that have found further expression in the book.

We want to thank Catherine Dee who brought equal measures of artistic judgment and conscientious organization to the massive task of selecting, procuring, and clearing rights to the photographs and illustrations that appear in the book. We are particularly pleased that the book will make it possible for readers to fully appreciate the fruits of her research, which otherwise fly by so fleetingly on the screen.

Showcasing Catherine's efforts has been the inspired work of the book's designer, Mary Parsons of Gibson Parsons Design. We are further in her debt for seeing in the photos and story the potential for a quality book and for recommending us to Elliott & Clark Publishing. We want to thank our editor Catherine Howell for her careful and caring work on the manuscript. And we want to express our appreciation to Carolyn Clark and Doug Elliott, whose decisiveness and enthusiasm made the publication of *Out of Ireland* possible.

Finally, we wish to thank our families—Patricia, Owen, Michael, Cara, Ellen, Frances, and Casey—for their loving support during the long days, late nights, and early mornings of work. This book is dedicated to them, and to our late friend and colleague, Dennis Clark.

—*K.M. and P.W., Charlottesville, Virginia*
March 26, 1994

Looking west across the Atlantic from Inis Mor, County Galway.

INTRODUCTION

ON JANUARY 26, 1870, a young Irish immigrant named Maurice Woulfe sat down in his army barracks at Fort Russell in the unsettled wilds of Wyoming Territory. Sergeant Woulfe wrote the following letter to his brother in Cratloe, County Limerick, in the southwest of Ireland:

Dear Brother Michael,

I received your welcome letter this afternoon. I was very glad to hear that you and all the family in Cratloe were well. Michael, I am in first rate health. I was never better in my life. This Rocky Mountain air agrees with me first rate. I have everything that would tend to make life comfortable. But still at night when I lay in bed, my mind wanders off across the continent and over the Atlantic to the hills of Cratloe.

In spite of all I can never forget home, as every Irishman in a foreign land can never forget the land he was raised in. Every stone, gap, and field in Cratloe and its surroundings are as clear in my mind as when I was home. I sometimes imagine I am on top of Ballaugh near Daniel Riordan's, looking over upon Cratloe and upon the old lime kiln where I used to play ball in my youth. But alas! I am far away from them old haunts. But still I imagine that I will see Cratloe once more. But if I do I guess all things will be changed.

I must close and remain as ever, your devoted brother,

Maurice H. Woulfe.

Write soon.

Irish immigrants arriving in America via 20th-century steamship.

Maurice Woulfe was only one of the 7 million men and women who came out of Ireland to America in the 18th, 19th, and 20th centuries. Yet this letter to his brother Michael captures the paradox of the Irish immigrant experience: "I was never better in my life," but "in spite of all I can never forget home."

Of course, every immigrant is a citizen of two nations, torn between the opportunities of the New World and their memories of the Old. But for few is this so true, or so poignant, as for the Irish in America.

EVERY IRISH IMMIGRANT'S STORY is unique and intensely personal. Usually, the details of those stories were stored away in the hearts and minds of the individual immigrants. There they were cherished, yet kept hidden for fear of reliving the pain of immigration or of conveying it to others who might not care or understand. Most immigrants revealed their memories and experiences, their successes and sorrows, only in the private letters they wrote to family and friends back home in Ireland, or in the memoirs they sometimes penned as legacies to their American-born children. Across the span of decades or even centuries, some of these documents have survived the processes of decay and forgetfulness. And, like Maurice Woulfe's torn and faded correspondence, they can bring those stories back to life.

Ships departing Queenstown, County Cork, the principal port of embarkation for Irish emigrants coming to America.

One of my earliest memories of thinking about America at all, was when my grandmother used to take me to the beach in Ballybunion in County Kerry. And we'd sit on the beach looking at the waves as the tide was coming in, and she'd tell me about the white horses. And she'd say they were on the way out to Hy Breasail, *the Isle of the Blessed, out beyond the western ocean. And that way beyond that again was Tír na nÓg, the land of eternal youth. And way beyond that again was America.*

Today, some 40 million Americans can trace all or part of their ancestry to those 7 million Irish immigrants. Likewise, nearly every one of the 5 million people who now live in Ireland has relations in the New World. This book, based largely on the letters and memoirs of Irish immigrants, represents our attempt to tell their history in their own words, to see their experiences through their own eyes, and to come to terms with their contradictory emotions.

THE ORIGINS OF IRISH immigration to the New World are buried in the remote past. In the sixth and seventh centuries, Irish missionaries left their homeland to spread Christianity. One of them, the legendary St. Brendan, supposedly sailed west across the Atlantic and discovered America long before the Vikings or Columbus. St. Brendan's voyage may be fictitious, but even today Irish folklore records ancient memories of mythical lands and journeys beyond "the western ocean." As folklorist and Irish immigrant Mick Moloney remembers:

Apart from these legends, the historical record of Irish immigration to the New World begins in the 17th century, when between 50,000 and 100,000 people left Ireland, most of them transported overseas as indentured servants. Others came as prisoners, Irish rebels and felons. They had been sentenced by British courts to long terms of banishment and involuntary servitude on the sugar plantations of the West Indies or on the tobacco plantations along the banks of the Chesapeake.

During the 18th century, Irish immigrants came in much larger numbers, perhaps as many as a half-million, looking for land on the frontiers of Pennsylvania, the Carolinas, and elsewhere in colonial America. Most of those who left Ireland during the decades immediately before and after the American Revolution were Protestants and came from Ulster, Ireland's northern province. Some were Anglicans, a few were Quakers, Methodists, and Baptists.

However, most were Presbyterians of Scottish ancestry, the so-called "Scotch-Irish," who brought to America such historically familiar names as Jackson and Buchanan, Wilson and Crockett. In the 1600s their ancestors had moved from the Scottish Lowlands to northern Ireland, in a migration organized by the British Crown and known as the Plantation of Ulster. Now, in the 1700s, oppressed by high rents and resentful of tithes and taxes, hundreds of thousands of Scotch-Irish left Ulster and crossed the ocean to what their Presbyterian ministers optimistically called "the land of Canaan."

After the American Revolution, during the 19th and 20th centuries, the Scotch-Irish and other Irish Protestants continued to immigrate to the United States and, increasingly, to Canada. But in the 1790s and early 1800s the Scotch-Irish were joined by a new and much larger stream of Irish immigrants. They came not only from Ulster but also from Ireland's eastern, southern, and western provinces, Leinster, Munster, and Connacht. These new immigrants would have distinctly different reasons for leaving Ireland and distinctly different experiences in America, in large part because they were Catholics.

Of course, even prior to the American Revolution, a small number of Irish Catholics settled in the New World. But it was in the early 19th century that Ireland's Catholics began their mass exodus overseas: to Canada, Australia, New Zealand, Great Britain, even to South Africa and Argentina—but primarily to the United States. During the half-century before the Great Irish Famine of 1845-50, perhaps a million Irish, about half of them Catholics, came to North America. From the Famine years until today, another 5.5 million Irish immigrants have come to the United States, the great majority of them Catholic.

These vast migrations of human beings were of enormous historical significance, for they shaped the future of both American and Irish societies, just as they shaped the lives and families of the immigrants themselves. For Ireland, the results of sustained mass emigration have

been devastating. Between 1841 and 1926 the population of that small island fell by half, from about 8.5 million to only 4.25 million. Many Irish have blamed what they regard as Ireland's social stagnation and cultural conservatism on the long, enervating drain of young, vibrant, and dissatisfied men and women. Even today, as the Irish playwright John B. Keane laments, "Emigration in Ireland is a predominant way of life."

For the United States, however, the results of Irish immigration were mostly positive. The Irish brought labor, skills, capital, and sheer energy to build the farms, cities, industries, and transportation network that laid the foundations of much of America's prosperity. Indeed, it would be difficult to list briefly the many Irish American contributions to the history of the United States.

By 1776 the Irish comprised at least 10 percent of the population of the Thirteen Colonies. And in many areas, such as Pennsylvania, they were active participants in the American Revolution. Eighty-five years later, more than 200,000 Irish immigrants fought in the American Civil War, the great majority on the Union side.

Castle Garden, a former concert hall in New York City, used for immigrant processing from 1855 until the opening of Ellis Island in 1892, the period of the heaviest Irish immigration.

11

A mother and son, Lisdoonvarna, County Clare.

The Irish, Catholics and Protestants alike, became prominent in American agriculture, business, the labor movement, religion, culture, sports, and politics. Irish immigrant farmers, lumbermen, and canal- and railroad-builders helped push the nation's frontier ever westward.

Irish entrepreneurs, including banker Thomas Mellon and mine-owner Marcus Daly, built many of the nation's giant corporations. Other Irish Americans, such as Terence Powderly and "Mother" Jones, helped create the labor unions that battled the corporations to secure decent wages for Irish immigrants and for workers of other nationalities. Bishop John Hughes of New York and Cardinal James Gibbons of Baltimore built the Catholic Church into the nation's largest denomination, while Irish Presbyterians, Episcopalians, and Methodists played major roles in shaping their churches in America.

In American literature and drama, few have analyzed the human condition and the American Dream more eloquently than Irish American novelist James T. Farrell or playwright Eugene O'Neill. In the world of sports, few have enjoyed greater success or popularity than boxer John L. Sullivan, the son of an immigrant from County Cork. And, finally, from the very beginning the Irish have been unusually prominent and successful at all levels of American politics, and no fewer than ten Presidents—including Jackson, Wilson, Kennedy, and Reagan—have traced their ancestry back to Ireland.

However, for the Irish immigrants themselves, and for their descendants, the results of migration were more mixed and ambiguous. Today, Irish Americans enjoy higher social status and greater wealth and influence than almost any other ethnic group. But the long history of Irish immigration is tinged with sadness, anger, and even tragedy.

Many Irish immigrants, past and recent, did not want to leave Ireland, even for the United States. Often they regarded themselves not as voluntary immigrants seeking opportunity, but as involuntary "exiles," compelled to leave Ireland by "British tyranny" and "landlord oppression." Many assuaged their fears and resentments with the fond belief that the United States was a fabled "promised land"—with "gold and silver [lying in] the ditches, and nothing to do but gather it [up]," as one young immigrant dreamed. However, although a few found their *caisleáin óir*, or castles of gold, in America, great numbers quickly discovered that such illusions were false.

John and Robert Kennedy, great-grandsons of Irish immigrant Patrick Kennedy, who emigrated from County Wexford in 1848.

Most Irish Catholic immigrants, especially in the 19th century, were poor and unskilled and had to begin life anew at the very bottom of the American socioeconomic ladder. Further, most Irish newcomers, particularly the large majority who were Catholic, did not receive friendly welcomes from native-born American Protestants. The society that these Irish encountered in the United States was not initially or automatically tolerant and pluralistic: the Irish had to make it so, through strength of numbers and determined efforts, often against bitter opposition. On both sides, but especially for the immigrants themselves, the period of mutual adjustment was long and painful.

Eventually, despite much collective suffering and many individual failures, the Irish Catholics were successful, achieving great prosperity and

Workers on the streets of industrialized America, Boston, 1910.

prominence in all walks of American life. However, the burden of their Irish heritage and the scars of the immigrant experience often proved enduring.

Even those immigrants who achieved security or success in the United States passed on to their children and grandchildren a heritage tinged with bitterness. Sometimes they expressed a certain skepticism or ambivalence about the so-called American Dream that had cost them so much to achieve. More often they channeled a strong resentment, or even a burning hatred, toward the British government and the Irish landlords whom they held responsible for having forced them to leave Ireland as unwilling exiles.

As a result, a profound homesickness was widespread among the Irish in America, even among "comfortable" immigrants such as Maurice Woulfe. Despite that homesickness, and as Woulfe himself suspected, most Irish immigrants understood they could never really return

"home" to Ireland—and very few ever tried to do so. Like Woulfe, they would live and die in America—and raise offspring who, try as they might, could never fully comprehend what their fathers and mothers had endured.

Thus, perhaps of all the different nationalities who came to the United States from Europe, Ireland's Catholics most forcefully and poignantly reflected the painful ambiguities of the immigrant experience. On the one hand, the Irish have risen with great determination to the heights of political, cultural, and economic life in America. On the other hand, they have nurtured a deeply felt longing for an often idealized image of old Ireland—the "Emerald Isle."

These seemingly contradictory impulses were passed on to succeeding generations, but they were most acute for the Irish immigrants themselves—for those whose lives transformed, and were transformed by, the histories of both their abandoned and their adopted countries.

To tell the story of that first generation, we must begin, not on the shores of America, but where the stories of Maurice Woulfe and the 7 million others truly commenced—in the green fields and rain-swept hills of Cratloe and a thousand other farms and villages of Ireland. For it was those farms and villages, formed by Irish poverty, religion, and bitter history, which shaped the hopes and fears, the resentments and aspirations, of the men and women who came out of Ireland to America.

The fields of pastoral Ireland.

CHAPTER ONE

THIS UNFORTUNATE COUNTRY

IN THE IRISH, OR GAELIC, language the act of leaving Ireland was most often described by the word *deoraí*. Deoraí translates into English not as "emigration" but as "exile." Similarly, when Irish poets and peasants described the act of emigration, they said, *"Dob éigean dom imeacht go Meirice,"* meaning "I had to go to America," or, "Going to America was a necessity for me." Thus, in the traditional Irish Catholic worldview, emigration was involuntary—the result of fate or force, not of individual ambition. And although the Irish language declined rapidly in the 19th century, the same sentiments were translated and reproduced in the new English dialects spoken in the Irish countryside—and in those Irish songs and ballads that portrayed emigration as tragic exile.

Of course, it was not simply their language that disposed the Irish to regard emigration to America as exile or banishment—it was the impact of English conquest and colonization on Irish Catholic society and culture. The physical and political consequences of that conquest can still be seen: in the ruined castles gracing the island's landscape; in the armed border dividing the Irish Republic and Northern Ireland; and in the murals and graffiti adorning the walls of Belfast and the other war-torn cities of the north. The psychological scars are less visible, but equally enduring, both in Ireland—and in Irish America.

THE RICH AND LOVELY valley of the Boyne River, in County Meath, about 50 miles north of Dublin, witnessed the birth and the political death of traditional Irish Catholic society. At Newgrange, impressive stone monuments, "passage graves" for ancient Irish chieftains, were constructed more than 5,000 years ago, long before the coming of St. Patrick and Christianity to Ireland. Not far from Newgrange is the Hill of Tara, the ceremonial capital of ancient Ireland, where the High Kings of Gaelic society were crowned and anointed. A few miles away are the ruins of medieval castles and of Catholic churches and monasteries, such as the Cistercian Abbey at Mellifont. Also lying in the peaceful river valley is the broad field on which raged the Battle of the Boyne. In that great conflict of July 12, 1690, the Irish armies of the deposed Catholic English king, James II, were defeated by the Protestant forces led by King William of Orange.

As early as the 1530s, English Protestant rulers such as King Henry VIII, his daughter Queen Elizabeth, Oliver Cromwell, and William of Orange had tried to conquer Catholic Ireland for reasons compounding equal measures of politics, prejudice, and greed. Again and again, Irish lords and chieftains, fearing the loss of their estates and their religion, had risen in revolt: under the leadership of Hugh O'Neill in the 1590s, Owen Roe O'Neill in the 1640s, and Patrick Sarsfield and the Catholic King James in 1688. Each time the Irish lords were crushed.

Irish faith and identity, a tenth-century Celtic cross, Arboe Point, County Tyrone.

Many of their leaders and followers fled into exile in Catholic France or Spain and were replaced as landlords and tenants by Protestant English and Scottish colonists. By the time of the last great defeat at the Boyne in 1690, even the Gaelic bards, whose songs and poems had once spurred the Irish into battle against the hated foreigners, had abandoned hope that Catholic Ireland could ever rise again.

In the years following their victory at the Boyne, the Protestant colonists and the British government imposed on Catholic Ireland a vast system of social, political, and economic control known as the Protestant Ascendancy. Nearly all land in Ireland was confiscated and given over to about 10,000 Protestant families, a few hundred of whom owned so much land that their estates and mansions dominated the landscape. Most

Catholics were reduced to the levels of tenant farmers, peasants, laborers, and servants.

Those Catholics fortunate enough to lease farms from their new masters were obliged to pay increasingly higher rents for the privilege of tilling the soil formerly owned by their ancestors. If they fell behind in their rent, or if their landlords' profits were better served by grazing cattle or sheep, the farmers would be evicted and their homes—even entire villages—would be leveled to the ground. In addition to rents, Catholic farmers had to pay tithes for the maintenance of the Protestant Church of Ireland. Although Catholics still comprised more than 75 percent of the island's population, the church of their landlords was now the legally established religion.

Even worse off than the farmers were the large numbers of desperately poor Catholic

Bellamont Forest, an 18th-century gentry house presiding over an estate of 5,300 acres, Cootehill, County Cavan.

subtenants and laborers who rented only a few acres, if that, on which to raise potatoes to feed their families. Driven by the need to raise cattle or cash crops to pay rents and maintain their own precarious position, the Catholics with larger farms could afford little pity for the peasants beneath them in the social hierarchy, sometimes oppressing them even more harshly than they themselves were exploited by their Protestant landlords. Nevertheless, all Irish Catholics, comfortable "strong farmers" and starving peasants alike, were united by religion and resentment against the Protestant Ascendancy.

In the late 17th and early 18th centuries, Irish Protestant landlords and bishops and the English officials who controlled the Irish government passed a series of Penal Laws designed to ensure the permanence of the conquest by impoverishing and degrading the Catholic population. These laws forbade Catholics to purchase land, to inherit land on equal terms with Protestants, to vote or hold political office, to engage in certain trades and professions, or even to live inside the walls of towns without paying special fees. Catholics were forbidden to own or carry firearms, or even to possess a horse valued at more than £5. For a time, the Catholic religion itself was virtually outlawed: nearly all Catholic churches were destroyed or confiscated, and many bishops and priests fled abroad or lived in fear of arrest and execution.

A hundred years later, by the late 18th century, many of the harshest of the Penal Laws were relaxed or repealed, and Catholics were allowed to purchase land and practice their religion freely. However, the Protestant Ascendancy remained firmly in control of both the soil and the government. Landlords and other Protestants continued to dominate Irish economic and social life. They enjoyed an Ascendancy guaranteed by the British government and enforced in Ireland by the constant presence of the Royal Irish Constabulary, Britain's only armed police force, and by as many as 25,000 regular British troops stationed permanently in barracks scattered throughout the island.

The British statesman Edmund Burke, himself of Irish Catholic ancestry, wrote that the Protestant Ascendancy had turned Ireland's Catholics into a race of cringing slaves. Certainly, the Protestant conquests, confiscations, and

Tenant cottages, Teelin, County Donegal.

Penal Laws had engendered a spirit of pessimism and hopelessness among many Catholics. But in the late 18th century, these afflictions also inspired new efforts by Irish nationalists to win Ireland's freedom by force of arms.

TO STAY AT HOME AND FIGHT for Irish freedom, or to emigrate and perhaps to prosper overseas: these were the choices that politically minded Catholics seemed to face in the late 18th and 19th centuries. Indeed, these were the alternatives posed by the stories of John and Walter Devereux in the 1790s.

The Devereux brothers lived with their parents and younger siblings on a farm at The Leap, a small crossroads near the banks of the River Slaney in County Wexford, in the southeastern corner of Ireland. The name "Devereux" (pronounced Dév-rixs locally) was of Norman origin. The family's ancestors had settled in County Wexford in the latter half of the 12th century and had enjoyed large estates and elite status until the English conquests of the 1600s had deprived them of their property. By the 1790s, John and Walter's branch of the family was again fairly comfortable, having succeeded in recovering some of the land their ancestors had lost. But they were still only tenant farmers, paying annual rents to Protestant landlords like the Alcocks, whose vast estate and imposing seat, Wilton Castle, dominated the local countryside.

As devout Catholics, the Devereux and similar families bitterly resented their religious and legal inferiority. And so in 1796, John Devereux packed up his frustrations and emigrated to the United States, hoping to make his living as a dancing teacher. His brother Walter, however, chose a considerably more radical course of action.

John Corish Devereux (1774–1848).

The democratic ideals and successful examples of the American Revolution of 1776 and the French Revolution of 1789 inflamed the imaginations of many Irish Catholics, as well as some Irish Protestants, with dreams of an independent Irish republic offering equal citizenship to both Catholics and Protestants. In the 1790s, these activists formed a new organization called the Society of United Irishmen and made plans for an armed revolution, initiating negotiations with the French government for military assistance.

The United Irishmen were especially active in County Wexford, where Walter Devereux became a local leader of the Society. Walter encouraged the local blacksmith, his neighbor across the road at The Leap, to forge long steel pikes that could be used as weapons by the insurgent farmers. But with the United Irishmen growing in strength and numbers, the landlords and government officials in Dublin became alarmed, and the British army responded with a campaign of cruel repression. They were assisted by the newly formed Loyal Orange Order, composed of Protestants dedicated to maintaining the Ascendancy established by King William of Orange a century earlier.

On April 1, 1798, in the midst of that repression, Walter Devereux wrote a hurried letter to his brother John in America:

Dear Brother,

It is the greatest happiness to you that you left this unfortunate country, now the prey of the Orange and Castle bloodhounds. Almost every county in poor old Ireland under martial law and the poor country peasants shot or hanged or bastilled without law or form of trial. Thank God that Irish men have resolution and can suffer more and will be free.

If the times are not settled before next August,

I certainly will then leave this land of tyranny and seek a land of liberty. But for a man here to promise himself a single day to live would be presumption, for nothing but God and the majesty of the people can save us from what every Irish man must and will shortly endeavor to crush to the earth.

Your ever loving brother,
Walter C. Devereux

On May 26 the Rebellion of 1798 began at a village called Boolabogue, only 15 miles from the Devereux farm. Led into battle by Catholic priests, the United Irishmen at first enjoyed stunning success. However, outside County Wexford their forces failed to rise in sufficient strength, and the promised French assistance failed to arrive in time. Less than a month after they began their revolt, the Wexford rebels were encircled by British armies and driven back to the town of Enniscorthy. There, on June 21, the United Irishmen were crushingly defeated at a place called Vinegar Hill.

Defeated, too, were the Devereux family's dreams of regaining the land they felt was rightfully theirs. Catherine Devereux, Walter's mother, apparently had not approved of what she later called the "wicked rebellion" that her son had helped organize and lead. Her response was understandable, for the events of 1798 left her a widow, grieving not only for the husband who died in prison, but also for another son, James, who perished at Vinegar Hill. In 1800 Catherine wrote to her son John in New York, describing the continued repression that County Wexford's Catholics were suffering at the hands of vengeful local Protestants. "If we don't get some relief, the Catholics can't live here," she lamented, and during the next few years she sent Walter's three youngest brothers, Thomas, Luke, and Nicholas, to join John in America.

While his father and older brothers had suffered for liberty in Ireland, John Devereux had taken full advantage of the freedom that Catholics already enjoyed in the United States. By 1802, after six years as a dancing instructor in New England and New York, John had saved more than $1,000. He used it to purchase a small general store in Utica, New York.

(Upper) Father Murphy leading the United Irishmen into battle and (lower) the defeat of the rebels of 1798 at Vinegar Hill, by British artist George Cruikshank.

The "Devereux Block" on Genesee Street, Utica, New York, 1905.

With the building between 1817 and 1825 of the Erie Canal, dug largely by Irish laborers, the little town of Utica began to grow. The population increased from merely 200 inhabitants in 1802 to 3,000 in 1820 and to 8,300 by 1830. Over the same period, the business partnership of John and Nicholas Devereux prospered, expanding from local merchandising into banking, manufacturing, land speculation, and canal and railroad promotion. John Devereux eventually became mayor of Utica, and both brothers became members of the city's elite. Yet they forgot neither their religion nor their fellow countrymen.

The Devereux brothers contributed heavily to Catholic charities and church-building. Nicholas established Saint Bonaventure College, run by the Franciscan Order, on land he owned near Buffalo. Likewise, the brothers began their Utica Savings Bank to safeguard the wages of Irish canal workers, and they helped large numbers of later immigrants from Ireland to begin

their careers in America. Thus, by the time of their deaths in 1848 and 1855, respectively, John and Nicholas Devereux had built a sprawling financial empire in upstate New York. Even if the Irish Rebellion of 1798 had succeeded, it is doubtful that John and Nicholas could have done as well in County Wexford as they did in Utica.

But what of their impassioned brother, Walter Devereux? Alas, the United Irishmen's defeat at Vinegar Hill had only confirmed Walter's premonition, expressed in his letter to brother John, that either exile or death was Walter's most likely fate. Walter had escaped death in the battle at Vinegar Hill. Now a marked man, trying to avoid capture by the British army, certain imprisonment, and probable execution, he fled to a nearby seaport. Family legend has it that he found a ship and sailed away, bound for the island of Martinique in the French

West Indies. At that point the story of Walter Devereux disappears into the vastness of the Atlantic Ocean, for neither his mother in Ireland nor his brothers in America ever heard from him, or of him, again.

A popular ballad of the period aptly described Walter Devereux's fate:

Well now that I'm titled a United Man,
No more can I stay in my own native land,
But away to America I must repair
And must leave all the friends of the
  Rambler from Clare.

So farewell to my comrades where 'ere
  you might be,
And likewise my sweetheart, sweet
  Sally McGee
Oh, the sails they're all set and the wind it
  blows fair
Oh, he's gone, God be with him, he's the
  Rambler from Clare.

Other Irish fugitives from the 1798 rebellion were more fortunate than Walter Devereux. Former leaders of the Society of the United Irishmen, such as Thomas Addis Emmet and William James Macneven, became prominent lawyers, successful businessmen, and honored citizens in American cities such as New York, Philadelphia, Baltimore, and New Orleans. Like John and Nicholas Devereux, these men became the first leaders of the new, largely Catholic, Irish American community that the first great waves of Irish Catholic immigration began to establish in the early decades of the 19th century. Moreover, this flight abroad helped enshrine the image of the Irish immigrant as a political exile, victimized by British oppression.

It was an image featured repeatedly and forcefully in Catholic Irish culture: in political speeches, newspaper editorials, clerical sermons, folk songs—and the letters of ordinary immigrants. It would color the natural homesickness of Irish farmers on the vast prairies of the Midwest. And it would seem to offer explanations for the poverty and frustrations of Irish laborers in the teeming city slums of the East.

Finally, it would inspire future generations of Irish immigrants, and their American-born children, to join Irish American nationalist organizations, striving to realize the lost dreams of Walter Devereux and the United Irishmen. For they would believe, consciously or unconsciously, that if Ireland were free of British tyranny, Irish emigration would cease and future generations would not be forced out of Ireland into exile overseas.

Nicholas Devereux
(1791–1855).

CHAPTER TWO

THE HUNGER

TODAY, A TOURIST IN IRELAND views a sparsely populated landscape dotted with farmhouses, each surrounded by its own green fields enclosed by stone walls. But the Irish countryside of the 19th century was filled with people.

Many Catholic peasants lived in crowded rural settlements called *clachans*. A few dozen, or even several hundred, one- or two-room thatched cottages were clustered together, surrounded by unfenced fields for raising potatoes and a few stunted livestock. Yet, these were not "villages" in the sense that we think of today, for they lacked the shops, markets, churches, public buildings, and other amenities ordinarily associated with village life.

The clachans, and those who lived in them, were desperately poor, especially in Ireland's western counties. Despite this they were the vibrant centers of rural Irish social and cultural life. As long as their potato crops were abundant, and as long as they could earn a little cash to pay their rents from selling butter or pigs, or from harvest work on nearby farms, the inhabitants of the clachans were virtually self-sufficient. Each clachan contained families whose weaving, shoemaking, thatching, and other skills provided most of life's bare necessities for the local community. Most clachans also contained the traditional musicians, singers, poets, and storytellers who gave life meaning and joy. Thus, in the clachans the Irish peasants could preserve their ancient customs and beliefs in a world apart from the "big houses" of their landlords and the ever watchful eyes of government officials.

Each one of these communities was located in a "townland," a small area of a few hundred acres, enclosing the scraps of land that its inhabitants rented, often at exorbitant rates, from the local proprietor or from one of his more affluent tenants. One of these townlands was Ardnaglass, located in the parish of Kilmacshalgan, in the far western county of Sligo, in the province of Connacht. The landscape around Ardnaglass was dominated by mountainous bogland, and nearly all the inhabitants were wretchedly poor peasants and laborers.

In 1825 the family of a farmer named Thomas Barrett left their home in Ardnaglass. They emigrated to an Irish Catholic settlement called St. Columban, in the forests of the Canadian province of Quebec. Thomas Barrett and his wife, Bridget, took several of their younger children with them to Canada, but left behind an older daughter, Mary. Shortly after they departed, Mary married Michael Rush, a laborer with a few acres of land, and settled down to raise a family of her own in Ardnaglass. Unfortunately, Mary Rush's decision to stay in Ireland would have fateful consequences.

(Facing) Overpopulation in the 19th century, Gweedore, County Donegal. (Above) Bridget O'Donnel and her children enduring the Great Famine of 1845–50.

THOMAS AND BRIDGET BARRETT were among the nearly 1 million Irish to leave their homeland and cross the Atlantic to the New World during the three decades after Napoleon's defeat at Waterloo in 1815. For Irish Catholics, Wellington's victory over the French Emperor was a double tragedy. Ever since the rise of the United Irishmen and the Rebellion of 1798, many had hoped that Napoleon's forces would defeat the British and liberate Ireland; that hope was now lost. Moreover, the end of the long wars between Britain and France ushered in an economic depression that ravaged Irish society, stimulating more Irish emigration in the 30 years after 1815 than had occurred during the previous 200.

The great postwar depression began to destroy the traditional ways of life in Ardnaglass and in thousands of other townlands and clachans throughout rural Ireland. The prices of Irish farm products sharply declined, which made it increasingly difficult, if not impossible, for tenants to pay their rents, tithes, and taxes. Thousands were evicted for defaulting on their rents, and thousands more emigrated to escape the prospect of eviction.

Irish cattle prices recovered from the depression more rapidly than did grain prices, and cattle-raising became relatively more profitable. Landlords and chief tenants responded by converting the small farms and potato plots into large pastures for raising and fattening bullocks for English dinner tables. But the tenants and agricultural laborers who had traditionally worked those plots were evicted from their homes.

The postwar depression also brought lower profits to many Irish industries, including the linen and woolen industries, which employed hundreds of thousands of cottage workers across the Irish countryside. At the same time, British manufacturers flooded the Irish market with cheap factory goods, further driving rural artisans into poverty. In the far northeast of Ireland the linen industry survived, and eventually flourished, by concentrating production in new factories in and around the largely Presbyterian city of Belfast. But virtually everywhere else in Ireland, cottage weavers and spinners of linen, like the Barretts in County Sligo, lost the precious shillings that had enabled them to pay their rents and avoid outright destitution.

Remarkably, despite these calamities, and despite the increasing rates of emigration they caused, the population of Ireland continued to increase—from 5 million in 1800 to 8.5 million in 1845. That growth was made possible by a dependence on potatoes, the only food crop sufficiently bountiful and nutritious to keep alive the millions of Irish who lacked any other foodstuffs.

In 1819, Edward Toner, an Irish Catholic immigrant in Pennsylvania, had made a fearful prophecy. "There is a destruction approaching to the people of Ireland," he wrote. "Their time is nearly at an end." By the early 1840s, roughly three-fourths of the people in rural Ireland were largely or totally dependent on their annual potato crops. At least 3 million of the poorest small farmers and laborers were destitute—living in squalor, pinched by hunger, and ravaged by typhus and other diseases. During the summer months, between potato harvests, thousands swarmed into the towns and lined the roads, looking to earn a few pennies or to beg for food. But the worst was only beginning.

Digging for potatoes in a stubble field.

EVICTION SCENE. 1767. W.L.

Irish tenants evicted from their home.

YEARS LATER, AN ELDERLY farmer described the strange events of August 1845:

A mist rose up out of the sea, and you could hear a voice talking near a mile off across the stillness of the earth. It was the same for three days or more, and then when the fog lifted, you could begin to see the tops of the potato stalks lying over as if the life was gone out of them. And that was the beginning of the great trouble and famine that destroyed Ireland.

For five successive years, the Irish potato crop failed, blighted by a new fungus. The result was mass starvation on a scale not witnessed in the British Isles or in Western Europe for more than a hundred years.

Unable to pay their rents, more than a half-million Irish men, women, and children were evicted from their cottages during the Great Famine—made homeless by landlords and strong farmers eager to enlarge their cattle pastures or desperate to rid themselves of starving dependents. Thousands of peasants starved to death in their cabins or by the roadsides, their mouths stained green by the grass they had eaten in a vain attempt to stay alive. Others crawled into the towns, seeking shelter in the government's

Sickness and starvation, Carraroe, County Galway.

poorhouses, which were soon crowded to overflowing with the dead and dying. Still others wandered about, frantically looking for food or work, spreading typhus and cholera throughout the island.

The worst year was 1847—"Black '47," the Irish called it—when hundreds of thousands perished from hunger or disease. But 1848 and 1849 were nearly as bad. During the entire period of the Great Famine, 1845-1850, more than a million Irish perished. Truly, as one priest lamented, "the angel of death and desolation reigned supreme in Ireland."

The suffering caused by the Great Famine was most acute in the west and south of Ireland—in townlands such as Ardnaglass in County Sligo. For poor families like that of Michael and Mary Rush, the only alternative to starvation was emigration. However, the Rushes had no money to pay for their passage out of

Ireland. A relatively few Irish emigrants, about 50,000, received passage money from their landlords. But for Mary Rush, as for many other Irish peasants, there was only one place to turn for assistance: to the parents or children, brothers or sisters, or other relations who had gone to America before the Great Famine had begun.

Thus, on September 6, 1846, the illiterate but desperate Mary Rush dictated a letter, perhaps written for her by the parish priest or the local schoolmaster, to her parents in Quebec, Thomas and Bridget Barrett, whom she had not seen for more than 20 years:

Dear Father and Mother,

Pen cannot dictate the poverty of this country at present. The potato crop is quite done away all over Ireland. There is nothing expected here, only an immediate famine. If you knew what danger we and our fellow countrymen are suffering, if you were ever so much distressed, you would take us out of this poverty isle. We can only say, the scourge of

God fell down on Ireland, in taking away the pota-
toes, they being the only support of the people. So,
dear father and mother, if you don't endeavor to take
us out of it, it will be the first news you will hear by
some friend of me and my little family to be lost by
hunger, and there are thousands dread they will
share the same fate. So, I conclude with my bless-
ings to you both and remain,

     Your affectionate son and daughter,
     Michael and Mary Rush
For God's sake take us out of poverty, and don't let
us die with the hunger.

Hundreds of thousands of Irish in North America responded to such pathetic appeals and sent money or passage tickets to bring their relations to the New World. As a result, during and immediately after the Great Famine, more than 2.5 million Irish emigrated, most of them to the United States. In only ten years, nearly 30 percent of Ireland's population left the island.

Thomas and Bridget Barrett, unfortunately, had no money to send to their desperate daughter. The Barretts' farm produced sufficient food for their family, but it generated no cash income. It was located far from any markets, the soil was thin and rocky, and most of it was still covered by dense forests. The Irish Canadian community of St. Columban was almost as poor as the Irish townlands its inhabitants had left behind.

As a last resort, Thomas Barrett appealed for help to his parish priest, who in turn begged for assistance from the British Canadian authorities. It was proposed to Lord Elgin, Canada's Governor General, that relief funds from the British treasury be used to bring out from Ireland Mary Rush's family and the other poor relatives of

St. Columban's inhabitants. Unfortunately, both Lord Elgin and his superior in London, Sir Charles Trevelyan, the director of the British government's Irish relief measures, rejected this and all other proposals for government-assisted emigration from Ireland. After all, wrote Trevelyan, "The great evil with which we have to contend, is not the physical evil of the famine, but the moral evil of the selfish, perverse, and turbulent character of the Irish people."

Tragically, such attitudes were not uncommon among the British officials who devised and implemented the government's relief efforts during the Great Famine. During the height of the Famine, the London *Times*, the semi-official newspaper of the British governing class, declared that Ireland's catastrophe was "a great blessing." It was a "valuable opportunity for settling," once and for all, "the vexed question of Irish … discontent." The *Times* advocated that the evicted Irish Catholics be permanently replaced by imported English and Scottish farmers who would be thrifty, loyal, and Protestant.

As a consequence of such prejudices, British relief in Ireland was grossly inadequate. Shipments of Indian corn were brought to Ireland from America, but British ships continued to transport large amounts of food *out* of Ireland to Britain. And some laws passed by Parliament during the crisis were actually designed to facilitate efforts by Irish landlords to clear their estates of starving paupers. To be sure, British Quakers and others worked heroically to save Irish lives. But many British politicians and officials seemed more concerned that too much charity might vitiate Irish character, of which the English always had a low opinion, than that hunger and disease might destroy the Irish people. These anti-Irish and anti-Catholic prejudices—

A "coffin ship" lost at sea between Ireland and America.

combined with British statesmen's devotion to the free market, to the so-called natural laws of supply and demand, and to minimal public expenditures—had lethal consequences in the Great Famine.

FOR THOSE IRISH LUCKY enough to escape by emigrating, the horrors of the Famine were compounded by the horrors of the Atlantic crossing. Emigrating to America by sailing ship was fraught with difficulties and dangers.

Most Irish emigrants first journeyed across the Irish Sea on the decks of crowded cattleboats to the English port of Liverpool before embarking on larger ships for their voyage across the Atlantic. However, landing at Liverpool did not guarantee the next leg of the journey. Some of Liverpool's inhabitants had an evil and well-deserved reputation for tricking the Irish out of their passage money or seducing women emi-grants into the city's notorious brothels. During the Famine years especially, many impoverished Irish never escaped the fetid dockyard slums of Liverpool.

Many of the ships adapted for the Irish emigrant trade were small, old, and unseaworthy. They were often manned by poorly trained crews and officers who cared little for the welfare of the passengers traveling in the bowels of the ship. Both before and during the Famine, sailing ships commonly put to sea without adequate water, provisions, medical assistance, or cooking and sanitary facilities. Voyages usually lasted for five to six weeks, but passages of more than twice that length were common, extending the misery of physical privation and outbreaks of disease.

Passage in steerage was a nightmare. The emigrants were crowded together in the ships' dark, dank holds, usually with only two square feet of space each. Only children had room to stand upright, and the narrow sleeping berths each held at least four people. These quarters were rarely or never cleaned. As a result, "the filthy beds were teeming with abominations, … the narrow space between the berths … breathed up a damp and fetid stench." Many ships arrived with streams of "foul air issuing from the hatches—as dense and palatable as seen on a foggy day from a dung heap."

Some Irish passengers came supplied with whiskey and tried to drink their way through the tedium and unpleasantness of the voyage. Most simply tried to remain on deck as much as possible, to escape the lice and odors below. However, when storms struck their vessels, as they did almost invariably on the North Atlantic crossing, the emigrants were forced back into the steerage. There they lay for the duration of the storm without fresh air, quaking with fear, praying, cursing, and vomiting, while the howling wind and crashing waves smashed and tossed their fragile crafts—sometimes bringing their dreams of the "promised land" to a tragic early end.

Irish refugees of the Great Famine experienced all the usual horrors of the Atlantic passage—and others that were exceptional. Many of the Famine emigrants were not only suffering from the debilitating effects of malnutrition before they embarked, but also carried with them the germs of typhus, dysentery, and even cholera.

During "Black '47," mortality rates among Irish passengers were as high as 40 percent in these vessels known as "coffin ships." Including those who died in the waterfront slums of North American cities, or in the quarantine camps, like Grosse Isle near Quebec, as many as 50,000 Irish died en route to North America.

ALTHOUGH WE KNOW from historical records that Mary Rush's anguished appeal for help went unanswered, we are less sure about her ultimate fate. We do know that the Rushes never reached St. Columban, for there is no trace of them in that community's detailed records.

Of course, it is possible that Mary Rush died in Ardnaglass, a victim of the Famine; between 1845 and 1851 the population of Kilmacshalgan parish declined by about one-third. If she did set sail, she may have died on one of the coffin ships or in the "fever sheds" at Grosse Isle, only a relatively short distance from her father's farm in the province of Quebec.

Steerage berths.

There is a possibility that at least some of Mary Rush's family reached the New World in safety. On May 15, 1847, the ship *Garrick* from Liverpool disembarked at New York a veritable tribe of 13 related Rush and Barrett kin, led by a laborer, aged 40, named Michael Rush. Was this the husband of Mary Rush (who was not listed among the ship's passengers) and if so, what had happened to Mary? In any case, the documented history of the Rush family vanishes on the New York docks. Thereafter their stories merge into those of the great, largely anonymous mass of Famine refugees seeking haven in America.

THE POTATO BLIGHT, the Great Famine, and the Famine exodus to the New World seared their survivors with vivid, imperishable memories. Fifty years afterward, one Irishman in America clearly remembered how, after the potato crop had failed, the "weeds had full possession of the soil, and … blossomed beautifully. [Their] yellow blossoms, glistening in the sun, … made a picture in my mind that often stands before me—a picture of Death's victory, with all Death's agents decorating their fields with the baleful laurels."

Some immigrants, encouraged by the Catholic Church, believed the Famine to be an act of God delivered in retribution for their sins. But many other Irish, on both sides of the Atlantic, laid the blame on the heartless tyranny of the British government and on the cruel greed of its Protestant landlords.

Their past sufferings in Ireland and their future travails in America would make the Famine refugees look back in anger, more convinced than ever that emigration was truly exile. In the decades to come, such sentiments would fuel the fires of Irish American nationalism and move later generations who had never known the Famine's horrors to donate their savings and even their lives to freeing Ireland from British rule.

Those sentiments would also inspire tragic songs that would reawaken bitter memories. Perhaps the most famous of such songs commemorates the suffering in Skibbereen, County Cork, during the Great Famine:

Oh, father dear, I oftimes hear you speak
of Erin's isle,
Her lofty scenes, her valleys green, her
mountains rude and wild.
They say it is a princely place wherein
a king might dwell,
So why did you abandon it, the reason
to me tell.

Oh son, I loved my native land with
energy and pride,
Until a blight came on the crops, the sheep
and the cattle died,
The rent and taxes were to pay, I could
not them redeem,
And that's the cruel reason why I left old
Skibbereen.

A woman evicted from her cottage.

John Roach (1829–1907) and (facing) Catherine Brown Roach (1831–1895). Refugees of the Great Famine who met, married, and raised twelve children in Freeborn County, Minnesota.

CHAPTER THREE

DIGGING DITCHES, PULLING SWITCHES

LATE IN AUGUST 1849, during the depths of the Great Famine, the families of Daniel Leary, Mathew Leary, and Denis Danihy sailed from Ireland to the New World. Irish-speaking tenants and laborers, they left the impoverished Kingwilliamstown estate that straddled the mountains between County Cork and County Kerry, in the far southwest of Ireland. Although they had been evicted from their tiny potato plots, the Learys and the Dannihys were among the fortunate few Famine emigrants who at least received passage money from their landlord. Thus, they arrived in New York City with some capital and were able to make their way immediately, via the Erie Canal, to Buffalo in upstate New York, where they found homes and work on the waterfront.

Less than a year later, one of their former neighbors on the Kingwilliamstown estate, Daniel Guiney, followed in their footsteps. Encouraged by the letters he had received from his friends in Buffalo, Guiney emigrated in June 1850. Like the Learys and Danihys, Guiney did not leave Ireland alone. He was accompanied by more neighbors, including John Keefe and his sister, Nonny, and Denis Reen and his wife Biddy and their children. This sort of group migration was not unusual. Throughout the Famine years, entire villages simply moved in stages from one location in Ireland to another in America.

A few days after arriving in Buffalo, Daniel Guiney and his friends collectively wrote a letter to those still at home in Ireland.

August 9, 1850
Dear Mother and Brothers,

We mean to let you know our situation at present. We arrived here about five o'clock in the afternoon of yesterday, fourteen of us together, where we were received with the greatest kindness and respectability by Mathew Leary and Denis Danihy. When we came to the house we could not state to you how we were treated. We had potatoes, meat, butter, bread, and tea for dinner, and you may be sure we had drink after in Mathew Leary's house. They went to the store and bought two dozen bottles of small beer and a gallon of gin, otherwise whiskey, so that we were drinking until morning.

Dear friends, if you were to see old Denis Danihy, he never was in as good health and looks better than ever he did at home. And you may be sure he can have plenty of tobacco and told me to mention it to Tim Murphy. If you were to see Denis Reen when Daniel Danihy dressed him with clothes suitable for this country, you would think him to be a boss or steward, so that we have scarcely words to state to you how happy we felt at present. And as to the girls that used to be trotting on the bogs at home,

Workers in a drain beneath the tracks of the Boston & Albany Railroad, West Newton, Massachusetts, 1896.

Irish patrons of Cundy Gallagher's saloon on Beaver Island in Lake Michigan, many of whom had chain migrated from Aranmore, an island off the coast of County Donegal.

to hear them talk English would be of great aston-ishment to you. Mary Keefe got two dresses, one from Mary Danihy and the other from Biddy Matt.
One letter will do for us all,
Daniel Guiney

To some newly arrived Irish immigrants, especially to Famine refugees such as Daniel Guiney, it seemed that the streets of America were paved with gold. And when letters such as his were received by relatives and former neighbors in Ireland, they helped dispel older, fear-driven ideas about emigration, and helped

persuade Irish country people that the United States was truly a land of promise. At the very least, in America there was work to be found and wages to be earned—and food to be eaten, in quantities unimaginable to starving peasants in Ireland.

However, the letters from America did not always convey the full truth of the immigrants' situation, as another Irishman in New York, William Dever, warned his relatives in north-western Ireland's County Donegal:

September 14, 1848

My dear Uncle and Brothers,

It's inconceivable the thousands that land here every week from all the old countries flying from tyranny and oppression. Wealthy farmers with their whole families are coming here and purchasing farms, some the best land in the whole world. Germans, French, Hollanders are doing this on a large scale.

But most of the Irish come out poor, unable to purchase farms. They work digging quarries, carrying brick and mortar in scorching sun up to the fourth stories of houses, in winter nothing to do, all their money spent. They are despised and kicked about. Many write home they are happy and wealthy, when they are of that class above mentioned. I heard friends of a young man in this city enquiring if John (Mr. Such a One) was not a banker here, as he wrote home that he was so and persuaded all his relatives to come join him. But what was he, think you? He was sweeper of the office of the bank. They were astonished when told so. And thousands are just like him.

Write immediately,
William Dever

Irish American priests and politicians continually urged immigrants from Ireland to settle on farms in the United States. But as William Dever observed, relatively few were able to follow that advice. Although the sons and daughters of small farmers and agricultural laborers, the Famine Irish immigrants were ill-equipped to become farmers themselves. Most of them arrived with few skills and little or no capital. Many were illiterate, and some spoke only the Irish language.

And so, most Irish found work only at the bottom of the American economy: the women as millworkers, servants, and cooks for America's expanding middle class; the men as unskilled factory laborers, miners, lumbermen, dockhands, construction workers, ditch-diggers, and builders of the new nation's roads, streets, canals, and railroads.

In eighteen hundred and forty-one
I put me corduroy britches on,
I put me corduroy britches on
To work upon the railway, the railway,
I'm weary of the railway,
Poor Paddy works on the railway.

Oh, I was wearing corduroy britches,
Digging ditches,
Pulling switches,
Dodging hitches,
I was working on the railway.

Workers in front of spinning frames in the Pacific Mill, Lawrence, Massachusetts, c. 1911.

Members of the Irish brigade of the Union Army.

For the most part, they worked in occupations where employment was never steady and where working conditions were always dangerous. In the middle decades of the 19th century, most Irish immigrant laborers earned less than $1.00 per day. Many could afford only a few years of schooling for their children before sending them off to work to earn a few pennies a day sewing shirts or selling newspapers.

Through such strategies, even unskilled immigrants sometimes succeeded in accumulating a little savings or property before they died. However, many other Famine refugees never lived long enough to enjoy the fruits of their labors. "It is a well-established fact," reported one Irish immigrant in a letter back to County Cork, "that the average length of life of the emigrant after landing here is six years, and many insist it is much less."

Thousands of Irishmen met an early death from overwork, industrial accidents, and disease. Thousands more died in battle while serving as soldiers and sailors in the American army and navy, for these were often the only jobs that poor, unskilled immigrants could obtain.

Many poor immigrants remained in New York, Boston, Philadelphia, and New Orleans, in the ports where their ships had docked. However, most dispersed throughout the United States in search of work. They settled where they found jobs, primarily in industrial cities such as Pittsburgh and Chicago. Others went farther west to San Francisco and to mining camps like Virginia City and Leadville.

Their first home was often a shack in a decaying slum on the waterfront or edge of town called "Paddytown" or "Little Dublin." After the Civil War many moved into newer urban neighborhoods, but their tenements were often as crowded and unsanitary as the shantytowns they had first inhabited. Epidemics of diseases like tuberculosis ravaged many Irish immigrant families. And infant mortality rates among the Irish were the nation's highest.

More than 150,000 men born in Ireland fought for the Union in the American Civil War of 1861–1865, thrust into blue uniforms to struggle and die for a cause, and a nation, they barely knew. Most joined the Union forces voluntarily, inspired by a combination of patriotism and economic necessity. Others were unwilling draftees who resisted conscription—sometimes violently, as in the New York City Draft Riots of 1863, the largest and bloodiest urban riots in American history. Many served in all-Irish Catholic regiments, such as New York's Fighting 69th, and perished on battlefields from Bull Run to Appomattox.

In late 1861, in a letter to his family back in County Carlow, one Irish immigrant described the war's first great battle:

Dear Father, Brothers, and Sister,

I suppose you heard all about the fight at Bull Run, where thousands of fine fellows fell. But one thing I know you heard nothing of, which is grievous to every Irishman, is that two Irish regiments met on that dreadful battlefield. One was the 69th of New York, a nobler set of men there was not in the world, who carried the green flag of Erin all day proudly through showers of bullets. The other Irish regiment was from Louisiana, also composed of good Irishmen who think just as much of Ireland. They opposed the 69th all day, trying to capture the poor green flag, and they took it four times but four times they had to give it up.

There were more lives lost over that flag than any one object on the field. The fourth time it was taken by the rebels, the poor 69th was so worn out that they were not able to take it back. But a man, a sergeant in the nearly all-Irish 79th regiment, cried out that the flag of his country was going with the rebels. He leveled his rifle and shot the bearer of it dead, and then he and his company made a bayonet charge and rescued the flag and bore it back in triumph to the 69th. You may imagine the joy there was on receiving it. Surely it bore the marks of war, all tattered and torn and riddled with bullets. It will be a lasting memento to the men that bore it through that terrific day. But never before was such rivers of blood seen!

I conclude in love,
Patrick Dunny

Members of the all-Irish Union Army regiment, New York's Fighting 69th, celebrating Sunday morning mass in camp.

Most Irish immigrants survived both the carnage of war and the hardships of labor. Like Daniel Guiney and his friends, they eventually found relatively steady jobs, settled in one place, and raised families. Despite their homesickness, they generally concluded that they—and especially their children—were better off in the United States than if they had remained in Ireland. Through their earnings and battlefield sacrifices, they had staked their claim to a new home.

For some Irish immigrants, however, the wandering that began with leaving Ireland be-came a way of life. They joined the ragged army of transient laborers who roamed across the face of 19th-century America. Take, for example, the story of William Murphy.

IN COUNTY ANTRIM, in the northern Irish province of Ulster and about 20 miles from the city of Belfast, was a small townland with the picturesque name of Rory's Glen. However, life in Rory's Glen was anything but idyllic for its impoverished inhabitants. In the early 1850s the consequences of the Great Famine forced a young boy named William Murphy, together with his

A Belfast slum, late 19th century.

Itinerant workers in a mining camp restaurant, Thunder Mountain, Idaho.

parents, brothers, and sisters, to leave their home.

The Murphys migrated to nearby Belfast, Ireland's only major industrial center, where William's father tried to find work in the linen mills and in the shipyards. When those efforts failed, the Murphys turned to shoemaking and settled in a slum crowded with other Famine refugees. There both of William's parents and three of his siblings soon died, probably of disease and malnutrition. Of the survivors, one sister chose to remain in Ireland. However, in the early 1860s, William and his younger brother, James, decided to emigrate.

William Murphy's first "job" in America was in the United States Navy during the Civil War. After two years of service, he became an itinerant laborer. He moved to Erie, Pennsylvania, in 1865; to Pittsburgh in 1866; to Chicago in 1867; to the Hudson River port of Poughkeepsie, New York,

in 1869; and then to Florida and the West Indies on a merchant ship. When William Murphy finally settled down with one job in 1870, his life was hardly less transient. He went to work for a company owned by Andrew Carnegie, building railroad bridges everywhere from Virginia to California.

Ten years later, William's brother James died in California, inspiring William to send these melancholy reflections to his sister and her husband in Belfast:

December 13, 1880
Dear Sister and Brother,

I have to knock around so much at the work I follow that I am hardly ever more than a week or two in one place. And I make up my mind to write home every place I go. But when I get there, I think

Washing and panning for gold, Rockerville, Dakota Territory, 1889.

this way: "Well, I'm not going to be long here; perhaps the next place I go I can wait and get an answer." And so it goes.

No doubt you think, why don't I settle down like other people? I have asked myself that question a thousand times. I have gone further—I have tried to do so. But when I try it, I soon get tired and the restless spirit gets the best of me all the time. The fact is, traveling is so natural to me that I might as well try to live without eating as without wandering around. But what difference does it make? Life is but a dream, and although I know that my last days will be spent in all probability amongst strangers, I almost wish sometimes the dream was over.

Don't think for a moment that I am despondent or downhearted. But just think for a second of the past that has gone, never to be recalled. It seems but yesterday since we were a happy and united family—mother, father, brothers, and sisters. Where are they now?

They grew together side by side,
They filled one hall with glee.
Their graves are scattered far and wide,
By mountain, stream and sea.

James, the latest of our loved and lost, laid him down to rest in the far away California. He like thousands more tried to find a fortune and instead he found a grave. But where could he find a more fitting resting place than in Lone Mountain? The last rays of the setting sun kiss his grave as it sinks behind the waters of the Great Pacific, and his spirit has crossed the Great Divide and joined the others in that better land beyond.

Dear sister and brother, may God bless and preserve you is the earnest prayer of your affectionate brother,

William

The notion of westward movement is deeply imbedded in the cultures of both Ireland and America: going west across the ocean for the Irish, and going west across the continent for Americans. And yet, in Irish and in other cultures, the notion of going west also means to die. Metaphorically, it would seem, the Murphys came to the shores of the Pacific to seek their fortunes, but only found another tragic chapter in their family's history.

Like hundreds of thousands of other Famine refugees, William Murphy was both escaping and searching—escaping from the poverty and disease that had killed his parents in Ireland, and searching for the steady work and decent wages that Irish society could not provide. Yet, as Murphy's letter suggests, the immigrants often yearned nostalgically for the homes they had lost, particularly if, like Murphy, they never really found permanent homes in the United States. Perhaps it was to these men that the old notion of Irish immigration as wandering and sorrowful exile most truly applied.

Union Pacific Railroad bridge construction at Green River, Wyoming, c. 1868.

Railroad section crew,
Indianola, Utah, 1900.

(Facing) Loggers on a
western red-cedar stump,
Deming, Washington,
1925.

(Facing) Crucible worker, Bethlehem Steel Corporation, Pennsylvania, 1910.

(Above) Crew of bridge construction divers, Kansas City, 1869.

CHAPTER FOUR

NO IRISH NEED APPLY

ON A SUMMER'S NIGHT in 1855, Thomas McIntyre, a house-plasterer from County Tyrone in Ulster, sat down in his boarding house in Boston. Weary and sore from his day's labor, he wrote a letter to his sister back home in the village of Donemanagh:

August 27, 1855
Dear Sister,

I know today you are all, or at least a good part of you, at Donemanagh fair. I am just thinking as I sit here alone of the times I used to have on those occasions. But there are no Donemanagh fairs here. There is nothing here but work hard today and go to bed at night and rise and work harder tomorrow. Nothing but work work away.

John wants to know if I still play the fiddle any now, but you may tell him that if he was here to put on mortar for one week, he would have very little notion about fiddling on Saturday nights. I sometimes think, when I go to my room without any one to speak to me, of the nights when we used to sit down by the fire and draw down our old fiddles. My meditations are not very pleasant. However, people need not expect a great deal of enjoyment when they come here.

Give my love to all my old neighbors and friends. You will scarce be able to make this handwriting out—I was just beginning to think that I had the trowel in my hand.

Farewell all,
T. McIntyre
Write soon.

Thomas McIntyre was one of many Irish immigrants who discovered to their sorrow that the streets of America were not paved with gold, but rather that the Irish immigrants were expected to pave the streets themselves—and for very low wages. The disillusioned letters that they wrote home could not stem the flood tide of Irish immigration, but they did spread a more balanced or realistic picture of life in the United States, informing would-be immigrants that America was not only a land of milk and honey— or of beef and whiskey, as Daniel Guiney had portrayed it. It was also what Irish country people came to perceive as a "land of sweat." In America, opportunities could be seized only by those who were able and willing to work much harder than they did at home—and willing to forego many of the simple pleasures of Irish country life that McIntyre ruefully recalled.

If letters like McIntyre's were not sufficient warning, young Irish who still came to the United States with naive illusions—"greenhorns" they were called by immigrants long-settled in America—soon learned some bitter truths.

(Facing) The "streets of gold," Fifth Avenue between 116th and 117th, New York City, 1893. (Above) Fair day in Athlone, County Westmeath, 1903.

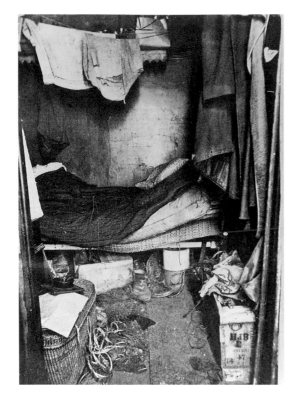

New York City tenement housing, early 20th century.

force to build the Chesapeake Canal in Virginia, they went to the local plantation owners and said, 'Rent us your slaves.' But the planters replied, 'No way, these slaves are worth money. Get Irishmen instead. If they die, there's no monetary loss.'"

For the Famine immigrants, especially, exploitation began as soon as they set foot on American shores. When they arrived, many Irish immigrants quickly learned that American seaports were inhabited by what they called "Yankee tricksters," who infested the docklands and tried to rob the unwary Irish of their little capital or possessions. Those who escaped the human sharks of New York City, New Orleans, and other ports soon discovered that their new American employers and foremen were often as harsh and unsympathetic as their old landlords in Ireland.

For instance, as Patrick Walsh from County Cork later remembered:

In the years 1851–52, the Troy and Boston railroad was being made through the north-eastern part of the State of New York. The contractors and others concerned advertised liberally, promised the finest terms to the working men, in order to bring together the greatest number. They came from far distances, and without the means of returning in case of disappointment. Accordingly, when the contractors found they had enough, and to spare, of laboring hands, they reduced the wages and kept on reducing until they brought it down to 55 cents a day. Against this rate the men went out on strike, as it would not support them, and matters began to wear a threatening aspect. At length, the legal authorities were called upon, with military force, to drive them off (which is always the custom in such cases).

I went to see the condition of those that remained, and in their "shanties," with the fierce wind howling through them, a scene of suffering presented

"You must work or starve," the new arrivals were told. "This is not Ireland, this is America, and there is no bread for idlers here."

Poor pay and long hours of backbreaking toil were not the only conditions that Irish immigrants had to endure in the promised land, especially in the middle decades of the 19th century, when the Famine refugees arrived. As the historian Dennis Clark has commented, "Whether they were women servants or men who worked in steel mills, these were people who were subject to the most fierce exploitation at a time when American capitalism had no governors and no constraints upon it."

The exploitation of the Irish by Yankee American society was based on fundamental prejudice against them as human beings, not just as workers. As Dennis Clark further points out, "When the builders of canals wanted a labor *itself which made the heart sick. All along for miles was one continued scene of anguish and suffering, as if some peculiar curse was chasing the unfortunate people of Ireland. Yet these things were noticed as mere items of news in the papers, without any comment, as no concern was felt in their case, being Irish.*

Incidents such as Patrick Walsh described were not uncommon. Often the wages of Irish miners and laborers on canal, railroad, and building sites were paid in overpriced goods, in devalued currency, or sometimes not at all. The injustices of the company stores and crooked scales in the Pennsylvania coal mining camps of the 1870s unleashed the fury of the Molly Maguires. This group of immigrant workers from the west of Ireland was named for an anti-landlord movement operating there.

Similarly, in 1859 Irish laborers in Jersey City barricaded the railroad tracks they had just constructed to protest not receiving their promised wages. In return, the city's business leaders and press condemned them as "animals" and as a "mongrel mass of ignorance and crime and superstition" who were "utterly unfit for the common courtesies and decencies of life." After a massive show of military force, six of the Irish workers received two-year prison terms for their affront to "order" and the "sacred rights of property."

As another immigrant put it more bluntly than had Patrick Walsh, the life of an Irish laborer in mid-19th-century America was often "despicable, humiliating, and slavish." There was

Black River Canal construction site, New York.

"no love for him, no protection of life. He can be shot down, run through, kicked, cuffed, spat on—and no redress, but a response of 'Serves the damn son of an Irish bitch right, damn him.'"

Irish immigrants experienced such treatment and prejudice from native-born Americans only in part because they were impoverished, unskilled foreigners. They were hated because they were Irish and because they were Catholic.

Most Americans prided themselves on both their British ancestry and their Protestantism. They also believed that Irish poverty was a sign of laziness and immorality, of ignorance and superstition—traits they considered inseparable from Irishness and Catholicism. Indeed, in the 19th century many Protestant Americans were convinced that the Catholic Church itself was the

sworn enemy of America's democratic institutions, and they feared that the Irish immigrants represented the advance army of papal aggression. Poor immigrants were not the only victims of Yankee, or nativist, prejudices, as John Blake Dillon, an Irish-born lawyer in New York City, complained bitterly, "The great majority of the American people are, in heart and soul, anti-Catholic, but more especially anti-Irish. Everything Irish is repugnant to them."

Because of such beliefs, the newspapers in New York, Boston, and elsewhere often depicted the Irish as violent and drunken, even as subhumans more akin to apes than to native-born Americans. Some employers refused to hire Irish Catholics and advertised for workers with the warning notice, "No Irish Need Apply." And, when Irish laborers did find work, their employers, foremen, and even their non-Irish fellow workers often treated them in what Patrick Taggart, a carpenter from County Mayo, called "an insulting manner," with "scurrilous attacks on our creed and country." Even Irish Americans who overcame poverty and prejudice, such as James Michael Curley, many times mayor of Boston and once governor of Massachusetts, were rarely allowed to forget what Curley had learned as a poor, Irish-speaking boy in the slums of Roxbury. They "belonged to an Irish Catholic minority who were despised socially and discriminated against politically."

On more than a few occasions, anti-Irish Catholic prejudices exploded into violence, sometimes with fatal results. In 1837 a mob of Protestant workmen from Boston burned to the ground a Catholic

Harper's Weekly cartoon by W. A. Rogers, with caption reading: "The balance of trade with Great Britain seems to be still against us. 650 paupers arrived at Boston in the steamship *Nestoria*, April 15th, from Galway, Ireland shipped by the British Government."

ST. PATRICK'S DAY 1867.

RUM. | BRUTAL ATTACK ON THE POLICE. "THE DAY WE CELEBRATE." IRISH RIOT. Th. Nast. | BLOOD.

The Irish stereotyped as a lower form of life in a *Harper's Weekly* cartoon by Thomas Nast, 1867.

convent in nearby Charlestown. In 1844 native-born Americans in Philadelphia rioted for a week, destroying many Catholic churches and much of the Irish neighborhood in the north of the city and killing at least a dozen immigrants. "The people here think as little of killing others as you would of killing the mice in a cornstack," wrote one frightened immigrant.

The large numbers and impoverished status of the Famine immigrants began to horrify many Protestant Americans. In the 1850s nativism became a nationwide political movement in the form of the "Know-Nothing" or Native American Party. The Know-Nothings controlled several state governments, where they passed punitive anti-Catholic and anti-immigrant legislation, and they seemed capable of winning control of Con-

gress and the White House. Some Irish immigrants sadly concluded that the Penal Laws were on the verge of re-enactment, not in Ireland, but in the "Land of Liberty."

In 1855 James Dixon, an Irish seaman in Philadelphia, wrote a letter to his sister who lived in County Wexford, not far from the Devereux brothers' old farm, warning his former neighbors not to emigrate to America:

September 4, 1855
Dear Catherine,

I hope the prospects in Ireland are good this year, respecting the crops I mean. I suppose the taxes will be increased to crush the poor people yet. However, if people can live comfortably in Ireland they ought to remain there, for affairs are becoming fearful in this country. The Know-Nothings have murdered a number of Irishmen in Louisville and destroyed their property. And if feelings continue as they are, on the increase, an Irishman will not get to live in this country. Even if people are poor in Ireland, at least they will be protected from murderers. I remain,

Your affectionate brother,
James Dixon

The Know-Nothing threat faded in the late 1850s, and Irish Americans' loyalty to the Union and their participation in the Civil War served to calm the fears of many Yankees. Indeed, Dixon himself moved to California, where eventually he became a wealthy rancher—as well as the lover of the wife of a British nobleman!—in Marin County, north of San Francisco. Despite Irish Catholics' economic successes and wartime sacrifices,

The sheet music for "No Irish Need Apply," an ominous lyric turned on its head by Kathleen O'Neil's spirited melody.

aversion to Irish immigrants and their religion remained common among Protestant Americans throughout the rest of the 19th century—and even into the 20th.

For many decades, being Irish and Catholic was still a stigma in American society, and prejudice continued to thwart the ambitions of middle-class as well as working-class Irish Americans. In the 1890s the members of a new and temporarily powerful nativist organization, the American Protective Association, pledged to refuse to vote for or even to work and associate with Irish American Catholics. During World War I, President Woodrow Wilson (himself the descendant of Orangemen from Ulster) and other pro-British Americans were deeply suspicious of Irish American

loyalties, fearing that ancient Irish animosities against England might cause the immigrants and their children to side with Germany. In the 1920s a resurgent Ku Klux Klan attacked Irish Catholics as well as Jewish and African Americans. And in 1928 the first Irish Catholic candidate for President of the United States, New York's Al Smith, was defeated in part because of such prejudice.

Despite all this, the Irish did survive and thrive in America. How they did so is the subject of the chapters that follow. But one can discern a hint from their response to the cruel slogan of discrimination, "No Irish Need Apply." They set it to music and made it one of the most popular songs of the 1870s:

I am a decent Irishman and I come from
Ballifad,
And I want a situation and I want it
mighty bad.
A position I saw advertised is the thing
for me says I,
But the dirty spalpeen ended with
"No Irish Need Apply."
Well, says I, but that's an insult, but to
get this place I'll try.
So I went to see the blackguard with
"No Irish Need Apply."
Some may think it a misfortune to be
christened Pat or Dan,
But to me it is an honor to be born an
Irishman.

As folklorist Mick Moloney has pointed out, in later verses the Irishman "goes on to beat the livin' daylights out of the fellow and to extract a promise from him never again to put up a sign that says, 'No Irish Need Apply.'"

At work in the culvert under Commonwealth Avenue, Boston, Massachusetts.

CHAPTER FIVE

THE EFFERVESCING OF THE VAT

AT THE HEIGHT OF the Know-Nothing crusade against his people, Irish immigrant Patrick Dunny wrote to his family in County Carlow:

December 30, 1856
Dear Father, Brothers, and Sister,

It's with joy I must say I received your welcome letter. In reply to your question about the election: James Buchanan is elected president on the Democratic ticket by an overwhelming majority. There never was such excitement in America before at an election, nor the Native Americans never got such a home blow before. The Irish came out victorious and claim as good right here as Americans themselves. I am happy to tell you that we are spending a very pleasant Christmas.
Your affectionate son and brother,
Patrick Dunny

Industrial Workers of the World organizer Elizabeth Gurley Flynn rallying strikers at a silk mill owned by a Mr. Doherty, Paterson, New Jersey, 1913.

James Buchanan is best remembered by historians as one of America's worst presidents whose incompetence helped bring on the terrible Civil War. But to Dunny and to most other Irish Catholic immigrants, James Buchanan and his Democratic Party were saviors, whose victory in 1856 turned back the tide of Know-Nothingism.

In the following decades the Irish scaled the political heights themselves, employing their numbers and political acumen to win power in many city and even state governments. In the process, they created bastions of opportunity in public employment where Irish applications for jobs would not be scorned but welcomed. At the same time, they forced America to become a more open and pluralistic society.

Many Irish immigrants to America would benefit, directly and indirectly, from Irish political victories, but few were as successful as Richard O'Gorman.

DUBLIN WAS AND REMAINS Ireland's largest city, situated on the east coast of the island just across the Irish Sea from Britain. In the mid-19th century, Dublin was still the seat of British government in Ireland—and the center of Irish nationalist agitation against British rule.

Living in Dublin in the 1840s was a young, ambitious lawyer named Richard O'Gorman. The son of a wealthy woolen merchant, O'Gorman had attended Dublin's prestigious Trinity College. But Trinity was a Protestant university, and O'Gorman was Catholic. When the authorities at Trinity required him to take a graduation oath that was repugnant to his faith, he refused. Instead, in 1844 O'Gorman joined a radical nationalist movement called Young Ireland.

In 1848, in the depths of the Great Famine, the Young Irelanders tried to raise an armed rebellion against the British government. But the Irish peasants were too weakened by starvation and disease to rebel. Young Ireland's efforts soon came to an abrupt and inglorious end—in a brief

skirmish with the police in a County Tipperary cabbage patch. Most of Young Ireland's leaders, such as William Smith O'Brien, were arrested, convicted of treason, and sentenced to exile in Tasmania, on the other side of the globe. Despite a £300 reward for his capture, O'Gorman escaped from Ireland aboard a fishing boat, as had Walter Devereux 50 years earlier. But whereas Devereux was never heard from again, Richard O'Gorman soon reappeared in the New World.

It was not Dublin that held Richard O'Gorman's political future, but New York City—the bustling financial and commercial capital of the United States. Through the patronage of Robert Emmet, scion of 1798 exile Thomas Addis Emmet, O'Gorman was admitted to the New York bar and joined the Society of the Friendly Sons of St. Patrick, an elite Irish American organization founded at the time of the

American Revolution. Despite the poverty of most Famine refugees in New York and anti-Irish sentiments, O'Gorman prospered as a lawyer and soon was more than reconciled to spending the rest of his life among what he called the "rush and progress" of American society. At least for himself, O'Gorman had discovered that neither his religion nor his birthplace was an impediment to success. Instead, only an individual's merit and wealth mattered in New York City. "We are a money-making people here," O'Gorman declared. "Talents are valued by what they will bring."

By 1859 Richard O'Gorman had begun to see another side to his hitherto idyllic portrait of American society and its effects on his Irish-immigrant countrymen, especially in New York City. He tried to convey a more balanced description of his adopted country in a letter to his former partner in revolution, William Smith O'Brien, now released from his Tasmanian exile:

January 1, 1859
Dear Friend,

I heard some ten days ago that you proposed paying a visit to the United States. Every man that can should see the United States. The progress of the country in all matters of material wealth is miraculous. There is the Yankee—wondrous energy, self-reliance, power of combination, readiness in the use of all his powers. He has rough and ready work to do, and he does it. The business of the day is to till land, cut down lumber, drain swamps, get rid of Indians, build railways, cities, states—and our Yankee does it with surprising speed.

And yet, there is another side to the picture—not quite so agreeable to look at. Not on bread alone does man live. Railways and steam ploughs are great—but not the greatest.

The tone of political morality is not high, and I feel myself intolerant and violent in my contempt for the governors and politicians in the United States. The whole thing seems to me a filthy pool of shabbiness, falsehood, and corruption.

New York is the headquarters of political corruption. It is here organized a sort of university for educating the rising generation in the endless variety of means for cheating the public out of their votes. A few leaders choose candidates, bring up their armies of voters, and the thing is somehow done as they command.

There have been various most energetic efforts at reform made during my time. The results were funny: great struggle, infinite speech-making, denunciation, detection, and great victory—virtue triumphant at last, new men rule us, and yet when we come to look at the bills for the year, we are robbed and cheated and taxed worse than before.

I am told this is the boiling and effervescing of the vat—the wine will come in time. I hope so. Time will tell. For the present, however, the thing is neither pleasant nor good.

It is refreshing, however, to find that in this effervescing process, our Irish countrymen have their share. In all political proceedings—primary elections, smashing ballot boxes, impersonating citizens, filling minor offices of all kinds, and plundering the public for the public good, in readiness to gull others or be gulled themselves—the children of our native land are eminently successful. The honest fellow I left behind me in Ireland is now owner of a corner grocery in New York and covets the post of alderman and scents plunder from afar.

I want you to write me at once and say when you are coming. Until then, goodbye my dear friend—

I am yours faithfully,
Richard O'Gorman

Richard O'Gorman (1821–1895).

The new urban America, Manhattan Island, New York City, 1876.

In fact, his letter's disclaimers to the contrary, Richard O'Gorman himself had already plunged headlong into the "effervescing vat"—or, more precisely, into the "filthy pool" of New York City politics. Well before 1859, O'Gorman had joined Tammany Hall, the city's chief Democratic Party organization, and had begun his career as an Irish American politician.

> To every party and every raffle I always
>   go, an invited guest,
> And as conspicuous as General Grant, boys,
>   I wear a rosebud upon my breast.
> I'm called upon to address the meeting,
>   without regard to clique or clan,
> I show the Constitution with elocution
>   because, you know, I'm a solid man.

Perhaps a heritage of political persecution and agitation in Ireland had prepared Irish Catholics to become expert political organizers in the United States. Another reason for their growing political power in America was simple arithmetic. As a result of the Famine, by 1855 nearly 176,000 Irish immigrants lived in New York City, and more than one-fifth of the city's voters were Irish-born. During the next two decades, Tammany Hall naturalized, often illegally, thou-

sands more immigrant voters—over 41,000 in 1868 alone!—to cement Irish loyalty to the Democratic Party and ensure victory at the polls. No wonder that boss William Marcy Tweed regarded Richard O'Gorman as a most valuable member of Tammany Hall.

During the Civil War, O'Gorman played on his reputation as an Irish patriot of 1848 and his florid oratorical abilities to rally the Irish in New York. He encouraged them to fight for the Union and to vote for Boss Tweed and Tammany Hall. His first major reward came in late 1865, when he won the first of two elections to become the city's attorney or corporation counsel. O'Gorman quickly became a pivotal figure in the notorious Tweed Ring, which looted the city's finances during the next six years.

According to the Republican, reform-minded, and anti-Irish Catholic newspaper, the *New York Times*, O'Gorman misused his position as New York's chief law officer. The *Times* claimed that O'Gorman authorized the payment to Ring henchmen of at least one million dollars in fraudulent claims against the city, while charging the taxpayers over $500 a day for his and his associates' legal services. O'Gorman also was involved in lucrative frauds involving the construction and maintenance of city streets. When public outrage caused Boss Tweed's fall from

power in 1871, O'Gorman intentionally mismanaged, and so helped to foil, the prosecutions of many Ring leaders.

Surprisingly, the collapse of the Tweed Ring did not ruin Richard O'Gorman's career—nor his reputation among the New York Irish. In 1871, the same year Tweed fled the city, O'Gorman gave Tammany's official welcoming speech to yet another group of exiled Irish rebels arriving in New York City. His private law practice continued to flourish, and, ironically, by 1876 O'Gorman had re-emerged into the political limelight as a leading spokesman for one of the local Democratic Party's "reform" factions. The *New York Times*'s personal hostility to O'Gorman continued, but neither its reiteration of old scandals, nor its charge that in 1877 he swindled orphans whose estate he had managed, prevented his election to a judgeship.

By the 1880s, O'Gorman was a respected jurist on the New York Superior Court, living at an elite uptown Manhattan address with his wife and five children, and spending his summers at exclusive Long Island beach resorts. When he died in 1895 his funeral at fashionable St. Francis Xavier Church was attended by a cross section of the city's native and Irish American political and social leaders. Apparently, O'Gorman's elevation

to the judicial bench had stifled even the criticisms of the *New York Times*, which eulogized him in death as a leader of his people and as a fine American!

Back in 1858, one of O'Gorman's former Young Ireland comrades had described him as "sharp as a chisel and equally keen in his race for money." Financially and politically, O'Gorman had won his race, although the course had turned out to be much more crooked than he had imagined as an idealistic and rebellious youth at Dublin's Trinity College. As O'Gorman had written to William Smith O'Brien from New York in 1859, he had long since left that "honest fellow" behind him in Ireland.

IRISH IMMIGRANTS were not responsible for the corruption and violence that plagued American urban politics in the 19th and early 20th centuries. Historian Dennis Clark has reflected that, well before Richard O'Gorman and the Famine Irish came to New York, the government of that and many other cities and states had long been notorious:

The celebrated Tammany Hall, 1868.

It was corrupt. Voting was physical combat. It was who controlled the polls, physically, who controlled the voting process. Political disputes were often settled in brawls—eye-gouging, ear-biting brawls. But that rough-and-tumble style of American politics gave the Irish the opportunity to become part of the political system.

Other conditions also paved the way for the Irish entry into American politics, especially on the urban level. Thanks to massive immigration and the enormous expansion of commerce and manufacturing, cities in the United States were growing at a fantastic rate. The legal structure of American city government was complicated and inefficient—virtually powerless to meet either the demands of urban businessmen for decisions that would favor their interests, or the needs and pleas of struggling workers and impoverished immigrants who desperately wanted public employment and assistance to improve their everyday lives. At the same time, the wealthy

Yankees—merchants, bankers, and lawyers who had previously run city governments—were abandoning the political arena to concentrate on their business enterprises. Into this vacuum stepped political machines such as Tammany Hall: party organizations that traded promises, charity, and jobs in return for the votes that enabled them to seize control of city governments and make them work.

For the most part, the machines and their bosses ran city governments to benefit themselves, and so most of the rewards of power went to men such as Richard O'Gorman. However, organizations such as Tammany Hall also provided opportunities for upward mobility to ordinary, working-class Irishmen. It was their loyalty to the political machines that enabled them to circumvent Yankee prejudice in the private sector and secure lucrative contracts and steady jobs. Those jobs included work done directly for the city as policemen, firemen, gas workers, and so forth, or indirectly for construc-

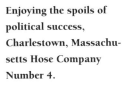

Enjoying the spoils of political success, Charlestown, Massachusetts Hose Company Number 4.

**Police Sergeant O'Hanlon,
Danbury, Connecticut.**

Political clout at New York City's St. Patrick's Day parade (from left to right): Judge E. J. Cavegan, Judge Daniel F. Cahalan, Mayor John F. "Red Mike" Hylan, Ex-Governor Al Smith, Judge E. E. McCall, and Clan na Gael chieftain John Devoy.

tion companies and other firms that did business with urban governments. Even Irish immigrants who remained poor benefited economically from the charity and protection extended by the machines.

Moreover, the Irish benefited psychologically from seeing some of their own people rise to power and affluence in a hostile society. They also benefited by seeing Ireland's green flag hoisted above city hall on St. Patrick's Day, at a time when the same flag could not be raised in British-ruled Ireland.

By the 1880s Yankee reformers were complaining bitterly of what one called "the Irish conquest of our cities." And by the early 20th century the rule of Irish Democratic bosses such as "Big Tim" Sullivan in New York, "Bathhouse John" Coughlin in Chicago, John "Honey Fitz" Fitzgerald in Boston, and the Pendergast brothers, Jim and Tom, in Kansas City only began to suggest the extent of Irish American political power. It was centered in city government but increasingly extended to the state level throughout most of the United States. To be sure, much public graft and waste was generated by their political machines. Many Irish politicos followed the example of Tammany Hall stalwart George Washington Plunkett, who chose as his epitaph the brash boast, "I seen my opportunities and I took 'em."

Yet, political corruption was scarcely unique to Irish Democrats. Non-Irish and Republican party machines in Philadelphia, Pittsburgh, and Minneapolis, for example, were equally notorious. Nor was Irish American rule of American cities always misused. Chicago boss John Coughlin earned his colorful nickname, "Bathhouse John," for building free public bathhouses for his city's poor workers. Al Smith, from New York City's infamous Hell's Kitchen neighborhood, turned Tammany Hall into a champion of housing, factory safety, and other reforms that improved the lot of working-class Americans. In turn, the liberal laws passed by Al Smith and other Irish Democrats on the state and municipal levels helped pave the way for Roosevelt's New Deal and Truman's Fair Deal legislation, which curbed the cruelest excesses of American capitalism and provided ordinary citizens with at least a minimum of economic justice and security.

Thus, both directly and indirectly, Irish political influence not only laid the foundations for Irish America's own rise to middle-class status, but also helped shape the entire nation's future in beneficial ways. In 1928 Al Smith's crushing defeat in his campaign for the White House demonstrated that the "vat" was still "effervescing": despite Irish triumphs at the city and state levels, most American Protestants were still unwilling to elevate the offspring of Irish Catholic immigrants to the nation's highest office. In 1960 the presidential election victory of John Fitzgerald Kennedy, "Honey Fitz's" grandson, showed that the process had finally been completed.

More than 100 years earlier, in the midst of Irish immigrant poverty and nativist prejudice, Richard O'Gorman had hopefully predicted the outcome in another letter to his friend, William Smith O'Brien:

May 17, 1857
My dear friend,

The destiny of our Race is to me utterly mysterious—for so much mental and physical vigor, elasticity and adaptability must have a destiny to fulfill. There seems to me nothing in the Irish nature to indicate a worn out, a moribund race. The moment it touches this soil, it seems to be imbued with miraculous energy for good and evil, so that something Irish is prominent everywhere, and you have to praise or blame, to bless or curse it, at every turn.

My own belief is that this northern continent will fall into the hands of men whose composition will be four-fifths Celtic. The descendants of the Puritans, the Saxon element, is physically deteriorating and will soon have done its work. A softer, more genial generation of men will be needed—more capable of enjoyment, more artistic than the Yankee. And our Celtic blood will just supply the want.

I am your faithful friend,
Richard O'Gorman

relatives at home. This was one reason why emigration became such a pervasive feature of Irish life in the late 19th and early 20th centuries. For, as one peasant in west County Kerry explained, if he did not emigrate to America, he would never see most of his relations again.

ON NEW YEAR'S DAY, 1892, the first shipload of immigrants approached America's new reception facility at Ellis Island, in New York's harbor. The first person down the gangplank was an Austrian man. He politely stepped back in deference to a 15-year-old Irish girl named Annie Moore, making her the first immigrant to enter the United States through Ellis Island. In at least two respects, this incident was symbolically appropriate.

First of all, it had been the Irish who primed American society for the waves of immigrants from many other lands who were to pass through Ellis Island into the New World.

And second, Annie Moore represented a feature of Irish immigration unique among all other immigrant groups. Of all the countries that sent immigrants to America in the late 19th and early 20th centuries, Ireland was the only one to send as many women as men. During several decades Irish female immigrants actually outnumbered males—in stark contrast to the migrations of Italians, Poles, Hungarians, and Greeks, among whom males overwhelmingly predominated.

In addition, the vast majority of Irish women who came to the United States did not come as wives or accompanied by parents. Nearly all of them were unmarried and traveling alone or in the company of sisters, cousins, or friends.

Two decades after the Famine, Alexander Sproule, a policeman in the northwestern Irish city of Londonderry, sent a plaintive letter to his brother in Ohio:

July 24, 1870
Dear Brother,

I have sorry news for you. On Thursday morning last, Ann, my eldest child, left here unknown to her mother and all, took all the money she could, leaving not the price of a loaf in the house, and started by steamer for Philadelphia. Perhaps you know some person in Philadelphia who could find her out. She is a smart, good girl— Whatever put this in her head? She is twenty-two years old, fair hair, clear skin, dark brown eyes, not tall. I know she is sorry for what she done. Please oblige me in a letter as we are in great trouble.

I am your affectionate brother,
A. Sproule

Although the vast majority of Irish women emigrated with their parents' approval or encouragement, Ann Sproule is typical in her determination to leave Ireland and come to America. Indeed, the letters of female immigrants indicate that they were much more inclined than their menfolk to view emigration favorably—not as exile, but as opportunity or escape. But why did Ann Sproule and so many other young women come out of Ireland, and why did they perceive emigration in such positive terms?

One reason was that employment opportunities in the United States were often better for young, single Irishwomen than for their male relatives, especially as domestic servants in upper- and middle-class American homes. As Patrick McKeown, a day laborer from Ulster, reported rather enviously in a letter from Philadelphia dated 1894:

The most of all employments, although fairly paid, are very uncertain, except for hired or, as they are called here, living out girls. There is always a demand for them as few native girls care to go out as house servants. Therefore it is left to Irish girls. Their wages range from three to four dollars per week and keep. They seem to be the most successful and save more money than any other class, as they are at little or no expense and get a great many presents if they are fortunate in getting into a good house. In fact, you can hardly distinguish a girl going to her work from a prosperous merchant's wife or daughter!

In view of such opportunities, it was no wonder that poor Irishwomen flocked to the United States—and that domestic service was their most popular occupation. Some Irish American servants amassed savings of several thousand dollars or more before they quit paid employment and married.

By contrast, in post-Famine Ireland it was exceptionally difficult for a woman to find work or a husband.

Back in the late 18th and early 19th centuries, women in the Irish countryside had been economically important, earning much of the

A shipload of "marriage-able women," as the newspapers described them, arriving in New York from England and Ireland.

FISH & VEGATABLE WOMEN

Fish and vegetable sellers in Ireland.

rent money through labor on neighboring farms or in spinning and other cottage industries. But by the mid-19th century, Irish domestic industries had declined dramatically, and the cities and towns offered women little employment or wretchedly low wages. Moreover, the shift in Ireland's post-Famine rural economy from crop tillage to livestock-raising sharply reduced opportunities for women to earn money in harvesting and other fieldwork. Irish parents still expected their daughters to work long, hard hours on farms or in shops—but without wages and with little hope for the future.

In late 19th-century Ireland, farmers' daughters could not marry men of their own choosing—and few were allowed to marry at all. Before the Famine, most Irish farmers had practiced what anthropologists call "partible inheritance": they had subdivided their holdings to provide farms for most or all of their sons, thus enabling them to marry and raise families of their own. This had made easy and early marriages possible, but it was a system that depended on farm families' willingness and ability to subsist largely on potatoes, the only crop that could provide sufficient nourishment to those who inhabited the smaller and smaller farms.

In this as in so many other respects, the Great Famine destroyed the old ways. The failure of the potato crop, plus the growing British demand for Irish cattle, persuaded farmers to keep the sizes of their landholdings and their cattle herds as large as possible. So, in the wake of the Famine, farmers adopted the pattern of impartible inheritance. Now parents willed their lands intact to only one son, and they usually required him to wait until he was middle-aged before they allowed him to take over the farm and marry.

Although most of the noninheriting sons emigrated, at least some could stay on as laborers on their more fortunate brothers' farms. But the daughters generally did not even have that option.

In addition, only those farmer's daughters whose fathers could give them dowries of money, land, or cattle were eligible to marry. Most farmers lacked sufficient capital to endow more than one of their daughters, which consigned the rest to spinsterhood in Ireland or to the emigrant ships. Under the dowry system Irish parents chose their daughters' husbands on the basis of economic calculations, not romantic notions. Instead of being free to marry for love, Irishwomen were usually "matched" with husbands who were many years older. By the 1920s the average marriage ages for men and women were 35 and 26, respectively. About one-fourth of Irish women aged 45 to 54 had never wed.

Finally, Irish parents' strict controls over their children's marriage chances were reinforced by the moral authority of the Catholic Church. In sermons and in schools, Irish priests and nuns admonished Irish youths to be dutiful and submissive, and to regard all potential occasions for romance as sinful, including even the crossroads dances that had once been a vital part of Irish rural life. Both priests and parents enforced a rigorous segregation on the young, separating males and females in church, in schools, in social clubs, even in the most public places. It was "a depressing sight," wrote one visitor to early 20th-century Ireland, "to witness lads and lasses walk-

A barefoot Irish colleen.

Women breaking clods with spades in a potato bed, Glenshek, County Antrim. (Facing) Women praying at a shrine inside St. Bridget's well, Moher, County Clare.

ing on opposite sides of the roads and incurring the ban of the priest if they even talk to one another."

It is not surprising that young Irish people fled in droves from such restrictive conditions, lured by bright lights and prospects of comradeship and romance, as well as better work opportunities offered by American cities. Young women, especially, left their homes for the social and economic independence that emigration promised. Their letters to Ireland only encouraged more of their dissatisfied sisters to follow their example. As one servant girl in New York City wrote to a female relation in County Wexford:

My dear cousin,

I am sorry that the priest put such a hard penance on you. You will have to come to the country where there's love and liberty. It agrees very well with me. You would not think I have any beaux, but I have a good many. I got half a dozen now. I have become quite a Yankee, and if I was at home the boys would all be around me. I believe I have got no more to say,

From your affectionate friend,
Mary Brown

SUCH A LETTER PROBABLY encouraged Mary Ann Rowe, from the parish of Dunnamaggan in

County Kilkenny, in southeastern Ireland, to make the trip to America.

Mary Ann Rowe's parents were comfortable, farming about 70 acres of rich land. They had no sons, but in 1887 Mary Ann's father promised his farm to her younger sister as a marriage dowry. Shortly thereafter, in the spring of 1888, Mary Ann emigrated to America and obtained work as a domestic servant in Dedham, Massachusetts, a small town near Boston. Later that year, she wrote a long letter to a close friend and former neighbor in Dunnamaggan:

**Mary Ann Rowe
(c. 1860–c. 1899).**

October 29, 1888
My dear friend,

It is not through any lack of friendship that I stayed so long without writing to you. I do feel so bad when I go to write to home, I don't be the better of it for a long time. I would never have left poor Dunnamaggan if I only thought I would be so homesick. I cannot banish the thought of home out of my mind. There is not a night but I do be dreaming about you or someone from home. I dreamed last night that little John was dying. I fancied I was looking at him and had the pleasure of kissing him before he died. I hope and trust nothing is the matter with any of them.

Oh, when I look back to our former days! How often we spent an afternoon on Sunday chatting over something funny. When I think of poor little Ellen and Jeannie, how they used to come out in the fields to where we used to be working, and poor little Mary Anne, how she used to call "John, John, John." How nice we used to put in the Sunday together with the little ones around us.

Yet I am living with a very nice family here in Dedham, Massachusetts. They are very nice people. I would not be allowed to go outside to put out the

clothes even when the dew was on the grass without rubber boots on me, my mistress is so very careful of me. And I am within two or three minutes walk from the church. There is a splendid church here in Dedham and three priests. I can go to mass every Sunday and to confession whenever I want to. Dedham is a very nice place and it is a country-looking place—when you look around, there is nothing but trees.

I must draw to a close for the present by sending you all my best love.

I remain your affectionate friend until death,
Mary Ann Rowe

If the combination of her extreme homesickness for Ireland and her enthusiasm for her new life in America appears contradictory, it is also typical of many Irish women immigrants. Ultimately, it is also revelatory. For if their letters to friends and relatives in Ireland were tinged, or even awash, with homesickness for Ireland, they also were unambiguously positive about the relative merits of life in America.

On February 28, 1897, Mary Ann Rowe was married to Patrick J. Sutton, of Providence, Rhode Island. Tragically, one year later, she died shortly after giving birth to a baby boy. Still, her nine years of gainful employment, her social and economic independence, and her ability to marry a man of her own choosing were all positive aspects of a life she could never have led in Ireland.

IN THE LATE 19TH CENTURY, Irish priests had counseled women against emigration, warning that America was a "godless" land where "rosy-faced, fair young girls, so pure, so innocent, so pious" would be "dragged down to shame and

The tree-lined streets of Dedham, Massachusetts.

crime, and to an early and a dishonored grave." Nonetheless, such dire and lurid admonitions could never stem the flight of millions of young Irishwomen who sought, and usually found, love, liberty, and money in the United States.

As historian Hasia Diner explains, despite warnings and hazards, Irish female immigrants were "undaunted and unafraid." It was well they were so, for most of the money that financed post-Famine Irish emigration came not from Irish men in America but from Irish women. It came from the wages they sacrificed to send home to Ireland—while still saving enough to create their own dowries so as to attract husbands and establish families in the New World. Thus, Irish women abroad not only sustained the migration chains linking Ireland and the United States, but through their earnings and their children they helped lay the financial and human foundations of Irish America's future.

Katie, Hannah, and Mary,
domestic servants, 1896.

(Facing) An Irish domestic
servant, New York City.

"Happy Laundry Girls," an 1891 advertisement using the image of Irish maids to sell Kirkman's Borax Soap.

A newsgirl at 23rd and
6th Avenue, New York
City, 1896.

TEELIN HARBOUR, CO. DONEGAL. 1452. W.L.

CHAPTER SEVEN

THE WIND THAT SHOOK THE BARLEY

AT THE TIP of the Dingle Peninsula in the far southwestern county of Kerry is Dunurlin, the westernmost parish in Ireland. It is also the closest to America. Lying off the coast to the west is the island of Inishtooskert, sometimes called "the dead man" because of its singular silhouette. To the east is the imposing mass of Mount Brandon, its summit usually shrouded in clouds. As the Irish playwright John Millington Synge observed with rapture in the early 20th century, Dunurlin Parish and the Dingle Peninsula present scenes of "indescribable grandeur."

In the late 19th and early 20th centuries, only a few hundred feet from the tip of the peninsula, was a clachan of thatched farmhouses and cottages in a townland named Gortadoo, "black fields" in English. There lived a young man named Tomás Ó Bríc—or Tom Brick, as he would be known in America—a fisherman and the son of a poor farmer. Decades later, in his old age, Tom Brick wrote his memoirs, recalling the days of his youth in the spring of 1902:

I was living at Gortadoo, between Smerwick Harbor on the east and Ferriter's Cove on the west, where I first learned to swim with the assistance of a boat oar and where I would dive into the waves as they were about to break on the sandy beach. But fishing in Smerwick Harbor was not getting any better, and, after receiving an occasional letter from my sister, Mary, in Salix, Iowa, I began to think about coming to America.

Tom Brick was one of many young men and women in Ireland's far western counties who began to think of emigrating to the New World in the late 19th and early 20th centuries. Despite heavy emigration during the Great Famine, which struck the western counties with particular ferocity, emigration did not become a permanent feature of life in the west until after another round of potato-crop failures and evictions in the late 1870s and 1880s. Indeed, among all of Ireland's inhabitants, the Irish-speaking peasants in the west, from County Kerry in the south to County Donegal in the north, had been most likely to view America not as the "land of promise" but as the "land of snakes." And they were most likely to perceive emigration as exile, or *deoraí* in their ancient language.

This longstanding resistance to leaving western Ireland seems remarkable, for the counties along the Atlantic Coast contain the poorest and most rain-soaked soils in all Ireland. Much of the landscape of counties Clare and Galway, in the region known as Connemara, is a granite wilderness. And County Mayo, covered largely by mountains and peat bogs, is so poor and desolate that it was customary when speaking of that county to add the phrase, "God help us."

Although the farms of western Ireland were small and destitute, their tenants had managed to eke out a precarious living by supplementing the produce of their potato fields with income earned

Traditional ways, Teelin Harbour, County Donegal.

Daydreaming on a rock in Ireland.

by fishing off their rocky coasts, by selling their illegally distilled whiskey, or *poitín*, or by migrating seasonally to work in the Scottish harvests. The farms were so poor already that it hardly mattered if they were subdivided, so most western farmers practiced partible inheritance long after that custom had been abandoned in eastern Ireland.

Life in the west was hard, but its severity was cushioned by the close ties among families and neighbors in townlands like Gortadoo. The lot of the western peasantry was made more tolerable by a rich traditional culture. Music, dancing, storytelling, and folklore continued to bind the western Irish—as they had once bound all the island's people—to their native villages. As historian Dennis Clark has remarked, "The

landscape was full of Gaelic names that were a thousand years old and that told of the myths and heroic deeds that were still talked about at the firesides in the evening."

In addition, the rigorous and seemingly unchanging nature of the western peasants' world bred a spirit of passivity, even fatalism, in the face of life's trials. Articulated, it expressed a feeling that it was better to stay and accept the hardships their fathers had endured than to chance a voyage on the stormy Atlantic to an unknown future in an American city. Further insulating the western Irish from what they called "the great world outside" was their illiteracy and the fact that the great majority, including Tom Brick, still spoke Irish as their primary or only language.

In the last decades of the 19th century, all this began to change, rapidly and traumatically, as it became painfully obvious that the old ways of life could not continue. Repeated failures of the potato crops, landlords' evictions, and Ireland's increasing integration into a British-dominated world market for agricultural goods—all forced the inhabitants of the west to adopt the new economic strategies and inheritance customs that already prevailed on the rest of the island. Although belated, their shifts to cattle-grazing and to impartible inheritance forced western peasants to send their sons and daughters to America.

By 1902, when Tom Brick began to consider emigration, three of his aunts and uncles, one sister, and one brother were already living in the United States. Letters from America and the spread of education and literacy were exposing the west to the allure of the outside world. "Study American history and geography," Brick's schoolmaster had told his pupils, "for that's where the most of ye are going."

The decline of old customs and of the Irish language itself produced in the west a widespread sense of despair and demoralization that, in turn, encouraged even more departures from what appeared to be a dying society. The old social and emotional links between the people and their communities were broken. As a result, by the early 20th century, western Ireland had the highest emigration rates on the island.

Tom Brick could not comprehend the sweeping forces that had transformed his world, but he understood their consequences. In his memoirs he described his decision to emigrate:

After bathing, I would lay on the bank over the black rocks, adjacent to the sandy beach at Cooltraig, and look west towards Innis Toushgart

beyond and wonder how Columbus ever got the courage to discover America. Here I am now close to twenty years of age, living with my father and mother and an older brother Shamus who is married and raising a family. He, being the oldest son in the family, naturally would fall heir to the landholding, such as it was. As for me, here I am with only the curragh boat and a string of nets to try to make a living. To get married and settle down under those circumstances was out of the question. And to sign up to learn any of the trades, which required five or six years of apprenticeship, without any pay and not enough to eat much of the time, that, too, was out of the question. And to make matters worse, the colleen I liked and loved was married, and given a dowry by her father, to a neighboring farmer's son. With all this happening at the time, it is making me think and decide on that venture to America. Why not take the chance Columbus did?

Of course, Columbus—like the earliest Irish emigrants—had sailed to an unknown land, whereas Tom Brick could rely on information and invitations from his relatives in Iowa and South Dakota. Nonetheless, some of the old customs and negative beliefs concerning emigration still flourished in western Ireland.

On the night of April 14, 1902, the day before he left Gortadoo for the United States, Tom Brick was honored with a unique ritual called an "American wake":

Tomás Ó Bríc, or Tom Brick (1881–1979).

The evening of the fourteenth there was a farewell party in the old Brick family house. There was singing and dancing, some drink, and lots to eat, such as we had. The large flagstone in front of the fireplace hearth took a terrific beating that evening while Shawneen played "The Wind that Shook the Barley" on his fiddle for the eight-hand reel for the four boys and four girls dancing it. The party remained late, and it was little or no sleep that night until breakfast time the next morning and time to make the rounds of the village to say "Good-bye."

Throughout Ireland, but especially in the Irish-speaking west, the Catholic peasants adapted their traditional wake for the dead to the leave-taking ceremony for Irish emigrants. It was natural that the rural Irish practiced similar rituals to celebrate death and emigration for, as they testified, there was "very little difference between going to America and going to the grave." When an Irish man or woman left home, probably never to return, "it was as if he or she

was going out to be buried." The songs, dancing, and drinking described by Tom Brick at his American wake represented what historian Arnold Schrier calls a "veneer of merriment" over the "strong undercurrent of sadness."

Sometimes the older women of the parish would raise a pitiful wail or "keen" in the Irish language, lamenting the emigrant's departure. As Mick Moloney remembers, such keens "would generate an incredible amount of emotion and release a lot of grief."

Many songs also burdened the emigrants with guilt and admonished them to send remittances home to their impoverished parents. Other songs expressed anger as well as sorrow. By the middle of the 19th century, most of the "exile ballads" sung at the American wakes were overtly political, blaming emigration on British tyranny and landlord cruelty. They burned into the emigrants' souls the conviction that emigration would never cease—and their sense of guilt for having left home would never be lessened—until Ireland was freed through their continued devotion to the cause of Irish nationalism.

Tom Brick's parents and neighbors accompanied him on the long trek from Gortadoo to the nearest railway station. In the little town of Dingle, he boarded the train for Queenstown, in Cork harbor, there to embark on the steamship *Oceanic*. More than 70 years later, he still remembered the "weeping and wailing and tears dropping there at the station by the parents, relatives, and friends of the emigrant boys and girls boarding the train that day for America." The Irish author John B. Keane, who emigrated from County Kerry some time later, described a similar scene and his own emotions:

I'll never forget till the day I die, the morning I left my native town. Young girls, young chubby-faced boys, all of them weeping, all of them reluctant to leave, but all being torn away by this merciless train, which was taking them to another world. I started to tap the train window and began to compose a song:

> *"Many young men of twenty said*
> *good-bye, all that long day.*
> *From the break of dawn until the sun*
> *was high,*
> *They left the mountain and the glen,*
> *The lassies and the fine young men.*
> *I saw the tears of every girl and boy.*
> *Many young men of twenty said*
> *good-bye."*

The song sort of broke in me—not broke out, it broke in me, you know. And it was the breaking of my own feelings. I was telling my own song.

"THE WIND THAT SHOOK the Barley," the reel the fiddler played at Tom Brick's American wake, could be taken as a metphor for the winds of change sweeping western Ireland, uprooting its young people and wafting them across the Atlantic. But if their departure left the countryside of Ireland depopulated, it was having the opposite effect across the ocean.

By 1902 America was alive with Irish men and women, even on the prairies of the Midwest. Tom Brick's sister found him his first job near Salix, Iowa, on a threshing gang run by a distant cousin named Long Mike O'Connor. Later, another cousin helped him find work in the stockyards in Sioux City. Yet another cousin got both Tom Brick and his brother William jobs mining copper in Butte, Montana, which had the highest percentage of Irish-born inhabitants of any city in

The forces of change in the form of a locomotive on a viaduct, Ballydehob, County Cork.

RAIL-VIADUCT.BALLYDEHOB.Co.CORK.10264.W.L.

**A community barnraising,
southeastern corner of
South Dakota, 1910.**

the United States. Later still, the Brick brothers tried homesteading their own farm on the Great Plains, where the howling of the coyotes reminded Tom, as he wrote in a poem, "of the Banshee's lonely croon."

For most of his first 15 years in America, Tom Brick lived and worked among his uncles, aunts, and cousins in a small Irish American farming community called Garryowen, in the southeastern corner of South Dakota. There Brick found a small, close-knit Irish world, similar in many respects to Irish American neighborhoods in Boston or New York, and remarkably like the one he had left in Gortadoo.

The Irish neighbors included the Clearys, the Murrays, the Malloys, the O'Farrells, the O'Maras, the Harringtons, the Joyces, and the Mulvihills. Then there was the Manley family, who built a great new barn and to whose house I was invited to attend a party. How they found out that I could stepdance, I do not know, but when Tom Manley started playing the violin, I could not resist. First on the list was the sailor's hornpipe, then with me doing the sword dance and others to the tune of "The Rocky Road to Dublin." I enjoyed the party very much, especially with the father, Michael Manley, who spoke fluent Galway Gaelic.

Although never very comfortable with it, Tom Brick spoke English more and more, instead of his native Irish. In 1914 he moved from the country to the small city of Vermillion, South Dakota. In 1917 he married a young Irish-speaking woman named Bridget Cavanaugh, who had grown up just a few miles from his home in Gortadoo. That same year, Brick purchased a small business on Vermillion's main street. As the town grew, his little ice-cream parlor became a thriving tavern and liquor store.

By the 1940s the eldest of the three Brick children was running the business, and Tom Brick was able to retire comfortably on the income from several real-estate holdings. Both before and after he retired, Brick was a faithful member of St. Agnes's Catholic Church in Vermillion and belonged to numerous Irish American organizations. Fiercely loyal to the Democratic Party, he even voted for George McGovern in the 1972 presidential election. In old age he continued to speak Irish with the dwindling number of his elderly Irish immigrant friends, and he still played the old jigs and reels on fiddles he made himself.

Although wrenched from the intensely traditional west of Ireland, Tom Brick had adapted successfully to life in modern America. When he died in 1979, just a few weeks short of his 98th birthday, there were fewer than 5 million people left in Ireland. Ireland's westernmost counties had scarcely 600,000 inhabitants, less than a third of the region's population on the eve of the Great Famine. In proportion to its population, the west had suffered more from emigration than any other part of Ireland. By contrast, there were more than 40 million people of Irish ancestry in the United States. Among them were the prosperous children and grandchildren of Tom Brick—and of innumerable other young men and women who had come out of the townlands of western Ireland to seek, and often find, their fortunes in the New World.

Bridget Agnes Cavanaugh Brick (1893–1939).

**Wedding portrait, family
of Samuel Allen McCarty,
Pocahontas, West Virginia,
1896.**

**Irish neighbors on an
excursion, Michigan, 1902.**

Workers on holiday from the textile milltown of Lawrence, Massachusetts, 1900.

(Facing) An "Irish pub," St. Louis Avenue, Duluth, Minnesota, 1875.

CHAPTER EIGHT

THE SPIRES OF ST. COLMAN'S

TOM BRICK WAS ONE of 4 million Catholic Irish who came to the New World during the late 19th and early 20th centuries. These immigrants experienced a much easier transition from Irish to American society than had their predecessors who immigrated before and during the Great Famine.

One reason was that the crossing itself was much smoother, eased by dramatic improvements in the quality of transatlantic transportation. To be sure, the sinking of the great passenger liner *Titanic* in 1912, with several hundred Irish immigrants aboard, demonstrated that crossing the ocean on even the largest steamship of the modern age was not without its hazards. But in general, from the 1860s on, the swift replacement of sailing vessels by steamships enormously improved passage conditions for immigrants. Even the poorest Irish passengers had more spacious accommodations, a secure supply of food and water, and best of all, a voyage lasting only a fortnight or less.

By the 1880s, newly arriving immigrants found a host of Irish American organizations ready to welcome and assist them. In 1857 one recently arrived Corkman had lamented, "Had I fallen from the clouds amongst this people, I could not feel more isolated, more bewildered." But by 1884 Owen O'Callaghan from County Waterford could report happily from Philadelphia, "Irishmen are pretty well-organized here under the principle of brotherly love and Chris-

A nun and her charges in a Catholic grade school, Louisville, Kentucky.

tian charity. This is a great place for societies, and 90 percent of the population belong to some order."

Irish-controlled Democratic party organizations or machines were eager to assimilate newcomers from Ireland into the political system and to provide charity and job opportunities in return for votes. But probably even more valuable to most Irish immigrants were the American labor unions.

Earlier in the 19th century, many labor leaders had feared that the influx of Irish workers would debase American wages and living standards. The Philadelphia riots of 1844 and other violent clashes had stemmed in part from job competition between Irish and native-born laborers. However, by the time of the Civil War, Irish carpenters, ironworkers, brickmasons, and other skilled workers had moved to the forefront in leading and organizing trade unions and in conducting strikes for higher wages, shorter hours, and better working conditions. In the 1880s hundreds of thousands of both skilled and unskilled Irish Americans joined the Knights of Labor, the United States' first nationwide labor organization, led by Terence Powderly, a son of Irish immigrants. Likewise, according to historian David N. Doyle, by the early 20th century the Irish were "incredibly dominant" in the leadership and membership of the American Federation of Labor. Their often bloody struggles

Millgirls marching in the Liberty Loan Parade, Lawrence, Massachusetts, 1918.

against exploitation won significant economic benefits for "greenhorns" arriving from Ireland—and eventually for all American workers.

Irish immigrants and their children also established a wide array of social, mutual-assistance, and charitable organizations. Nearly every American city and industrial town had a full range of Irish American social clubs, often catering to immigrants from specific counties in Ireland, that held dances, picnics, raffles, and athletic contests. Irish American benevolent societies provided unemployment benefits and funeral expenses to immigrant workers and their families. Other organizations encouraged Irish immigrants to avoid the dangers of drink. Still others were designed to preserve and promote Irish identity in the United States. By the turn of the century, many of these societies had become large national organizations, such as the Irish Catholic Benevolent Union and the Ancient Order of Hibernians. By 1908 the latter alone

claimed nearly 200,000 Irish men and women as members.

Every March 17th, all these societies—joined by Irish Democratic politicians and Catholic clergy—proclaimed their pride and power in huge parades honoring St. Patrick. For ordinary Irish immigrants, these parades heightened their sense of ethnic identity and their emotional links to their homeland. "In the emotion I felt," recalled Batt O'Connor from County Kerry, "walking as one of that vast crowd of Irish emigrants celebrating our national festival, I awoke to the full consciousness of my love for my country."

Such celebrations also announced an advance in status for Irish Americans in their adopted country. William Downes, a dry-goods salesman in Brooklyn, explained to a friend in County Limerick that the middle-class Irish Americans who usually led these ethnic organizations and parades designed them as vehicles to uplift and reform the immigrants into "good Americans" whose behavior would be immune from criticism.

October 13, 1887

My dear old comrade,

It is with feelings of regret that I acknowledge my negligence in delaying to answer your highly esteemed letter. I was on a temperance crusade in Philadelphia. It was a national convention of the Catholic Total Abstinence Union, comprising delegates from all the societies in America. In the procession there were over 70,000 men. I was honored by being elected Provincial Vice-President of New York, Brooklyn, and New Jersey.

My Sundays are all devoted to temperance. I go around from one society to another and enjoy myself in that way. I got disgusted with the drinking habits practiced here by too many of our country people. I know a number of people from home who have become sots, through the terrible influence of the intoxicating cup.

America is no place for a man who intends to tipple. The Irish people should never touch liquor or beer in America, that is, if they are desirous of becoming good citizens, and reflect credit on the land that bore them.

This is why I have devoted so much of my time to the question of total abstinence. It is the golden lever which will guide our weak machinery to a successful goal.

Yours sincerely,

W. H. Downes

William Downes's Total Abstinence Union, like the Ancient Order of Hibernians and most other Irish American organizations, was closely affiliated with the Catholic Church. Of all the institutions that eased the immigrants' transition between Irish and American life, the Catholic Church was the most important. "We have changed the clime," declared one Irishman in America, "but not the faith." In fact, during the course of the 19th century the religious practices and beliefs of Irish Catholics, both in Ireland and in the United States, had changed rather dramatically.

The community band, Beaver Island, Lake Michigan, 1915.

Members of the Knights of Labor, a heavily Irish trade union.

(Facing) The Monaghan Men's Dancing Class learning the social skills of the American middle class.

**Traditional mummers
called "wren boys,"
pre-Christian in origin,
County Limerick.**

ONLY A FEW MILES from Tom Brick's home in South Dakota, just north of Vermillion and west of Garryowen, was a hill called Spirit Mound, which the defeated and displaced Sioux Indians had believed was haunted by a mysterious and malicious race of "little people." Tom Brick must have appreciated this continuity with his Irish past, for despite their devout Catholicism, he and many other Irish immigrants still believed in fairies.

Today, the people of Ireland are perhaps the world's most faithfully practicing Catholics, with the highest rates of church attendance anywhere. Yet it was not always so.

Prior to the Great Famine most Irish country people were not practicing Catholics in the formal ways prescribed by their priests and bishops. Relatively few Irish attended mass or confession regularly, particularly in southern and western Ireland where chapels and clergy were scarce. In those and other regions, most peasants expressed their devotion through religious customs outside the Church, such as pilgrimages to holy wells. Often these sites were thousands of years old and had been sacred to the ancient Irish who had worshiped pagan deities long before St. Patrick brought Christianity to Ireland.

Alongside the official presence and doctrines of the Catholic Church, an entire system of traditional beliefs and customs still flourished, overlain by only a thin veneer of formal Christianity. Irish country people still celebrated archaic spring and harvest festivals, practiced magical cures to combat sickness and witchcraft, and, most prevalent of all, believed in the existence of fairies.

Usually unseen and unheard, the fairies supposedly inhabited abandoned farmhouses, ancient ruins, hills, and trees. Sometimes, it was believed, they performed beneficial functions, protecting the human inhabitants of their realms against English oppression or, like the banshees, warning of approaching death by their unearthly wails. Usually, though, the fairies were considered malevolent. Unless bribed by gifts or rituals, they would blight the peasants' crops, sicken their livestock, or even steal healthy infants out of their cribs, leaving dead "changelings" in their place.

Although popular belief in fairies remained strong well into the 20th century, the old customs began to disappear with the spread of commerce and literacy in the middle of the 19th century. Bishops and priests had long attempted, with increasing success, to uproot these remnants of paganism among Ireland's Catholics. The cataclysm of the Great Famine convinced most peasants not only that the old beliefs were ineffectual in staving off disaster, but that God had punished them for their wicked resistance to the Church's teachings. After the Famine, faced with the steady decline of their traditional language and culture, Ireland's Catholics turned more often to their Church for consolation and leadership.

And the Church responded. Irish bishops and priests raised millions of pounds at home and abroad to construct hundreds of new chapels and cathedrals that dwarfed the poverty of the surrounding villages. They also trained thousands of new priests and nuns; organized their

A group of priests attend the blessing of a shrine, County Leitrim.

Mary and John Hickey, the children of immigrants from County Kerry, making their First Holy Communion in America, 1910.

Irish emigrants' "divine mission" to carry and transplant a devout Catholicism overseas.

So by 1902, when Tom Brick and his fellow passengers sailed out of Queenstown, the principal embarkation point for emigrants to America, the last Irish landmarks they saw on the horizon were the tall spires of St. Colman's Cathedral, reminding them, it was said, of their obligations to Holy Mother Church in the New World.

Upon arriving in New York City, they found the equally imposing towers of St. Patrick's Cathedral soaring above fashionable Fifth Avenue, symbolizing the religious devotion of Irish Americans, as well as their rise to social and economic respectability. The fairies might still exist in the recesses of Tom Brick's mind, but they could never compete with such monuments to faith, wealth, and power.

EARLIER IN THE 19TH CENTURY, before the great wave of Famine Irish immigrants in the 1840s and 1850s, Catholicism in the United States was largely invisible. Catholics were few in number, and they valued their invisibility as a defense against Protestant American prejudice. Most American priests and bishops were of English or French derivation and were appalled by the floods of Irish immigrants whose poverty and customs threatened to expose the Church to Protestant scorn.

At mid-century a pious Irish immigrant in New York City complained that "the Roman Catholic religion is not carried to its full extent here as in old Ireland." Only a few decades later and a few miles up the Hudson River in the small parish of Barrytown, Arthur Quin from County Tyrone told quite a different story:

adult parishioners into temperance societies, confraternities, and sodalities; and came to dominate the public education of Ireland's Catholic youth.

By the end of the century, the Irish Catholic Church's "devotional revolution" was complete. The priests and bishops had created what they called a "Holy Ireland," preaching that it was the

Dear brother and sister,

There is a great change for the better since we came here. In this place about ten years ago there was no church nor no priest. But it was the greatest crowd of people ever was seen in Barrytown the day the corner-stone was laid, and now we have our new church finished and we had the first mass that was said in it on Christmas day. Now we have mass every Sunday and we can mind our duty as well here as we can in Ireland. The clergy is very strict about the children's religion. They have Sunday school every Sunday. No more at present.

Your affectionate brother,
Arthur Quin

The arrival of the Famine Irish in droves radically transformed the Catholic Church in America. Led by aggressive, Irish-born bishops such as John Hughes of New York, the Church in the United States expanded even more rapidly and dramatically than in Ireland. Thousands of new churches were constructed. Tens of thousands of new priests and members of teaching and charitable orders were imported from Ireland or trained in America. A comprehensive system of parochial education, from primary schools to universities such as Georgetown and Notre Dame, was created. By the 20th century, the Catholic Church had become the nation's largest religious denomination. When millions of other European, French Canadian, and Latin American Catholics came to the United States, they found a Church ready to receive them and a Church largely dominated by the Irish.

The strength, affluence, and respectability of the Church in America was of great value to Irish immigrants. The Church provided not only a place of worship, but a source of education,

Catholics praying in Holy Cross Cemetery, following word of miracles taking place there, Malden, Massachusetts, 1929.

Charter Members of the Fourth Degree, Knights of Columbus, 1900.

recreation, business, and social life. The Church became a bulwark against the animosity of Protestant Americans, providing comfort and protection for Irish immigrants even as it worked to enhance their status in American life. As one Irish American woman wrote to her friend in Ireland, "You will not fret for being in a strange country if you mind your duty to God and go to your priest and consult with him." Their strong religious faith provided solace to poor laborers such as Michael Kilcran from County Leitrim, who reflected that the sun that shone on his brutal, poorly paid work in the Chicago stockyards was "just the same sun as used to shine in Ireland, under the guidance and control of the same one God—ruler of my destiny."

Thus, a common Catholicism bridged the ocean between Ireland and the United States, between the spires of St. Colman's and St. Patrick's cathedrals, helping to shape and perpetuate Irish identity on both sides of the

Atlantic. "Take an average Irishman," declared an Irish priest in America. "I don't care where you find him—and you will find that the very first principle in his mind is, 'I am not an Englishman, because I am a Catholic.'"

AS HISTORIAN Dennis Clark has commented, the Irish who came to the United States at the end of the 19th and the beginning of the 20th century had many resources. Millions of Irish immigrants, including many of their own relatives, had preceded them, establishing Irish American neighborhoods, communities, and a network of political clubs, labor unions, churches, and other organizations. That network "reached all the way down to landladies who kept an eye on immigrant daughters and sons, kept them from drinking, and kept them out of trouble."

As one immigrant wrote, by the turn of the century, Irish immigration was no longer "like going into a city where you don't know anybody." Instead, wherever he or she went in the United States, a newly arrived Irish immigrant could find "A Typical Tipperary":

> There's a typical Tipperary, a typical
>   Dublin Bay,
> Well, a typical County Kerry in the
>   good old U.S.A.
> Although you're many miles, from where
>   the shamrock grows,
> You'll find an Irishman no matter
>   where you go …
> If you want an Irish treat,
> You'll march up and down Delancey Street,
> You'll think that you were home in Ireland.

A procession through Roxbury, Massachusetts, 1954.

CHAPTER NINE

REVENGE FOR SKIBBEREEN

IN THE OLD FAMINE SONG "Skibbereen," several early verses are sung by a father to his son describing the horrors of the famine and the cruelties of the English landlords. The final verse of the song is the response of the son, now living in America:

> Oh, father dear, the day will come when
> vengeance loud will call,
> And Erin's sons will rally round and battle
> one and all.
> I'll be the man to lead the van beneath
> our flag of green,
> And loud and high will raise the cry,
> "Revenge for Skibbereen!"

Despite their success in American society, many Irish Catholic immigrants still believed that their emigration had been involuntary, caused by British and landlord oppression. The memories, stories and songs of the Great Famine seemed to confirm the old belief that emigration was "exile" and warranted a terrible retribution.

NEAR THE COAST of County Cork, only an hour's drive from Skibbereen, is the parish and village of Killeagh. In 1871 Timothy Cashman, the son of an Irish-speaking farm laborer, was born there. In the late 19th century, life for the Cashmans and for other poor, landless laborers was almost as hard as it had been before the Famine. Most still lived in tiny thatched hovels, subsisted largely on potatoes, and rarely wore shoes. They also suffered harsh exploitation from their employers. Years later, Tim Cashman bitterly recalled both the tyranny of the local Protestant landlords and the equally scornful treatment his family and other laborers had received from wealthy Catholic farmers and shopkeepers.

There were compensations, however, even for poor youths such as Tim Cashman. Near the village of Killeagh was a lovely oak forest called Glenbower Wood, where the young men and women of the parish would gather in the evenings, removed from the watchful eyes of employers, parents, and priests. In his old age, Tim Cashman relived in memory the best days of his life, spent in Glenbower's ancient groves:

Sunday afternoons in summer time the boys and girls congregated at a cross-roads in the district and danced away the time until sundown. A piper came there from some distance to provide the music, also a violin player. Besides the dancing, all kinds of sports were indulged—running, jumping, bowl-playing, and so forth. In winter the neighbors would gather to one another's fireside during the long evenings and begin story-telling of Ireland's past. The legends of Fionn McCumhal's warriors and all other phases of Ireland's lore were laid bare to the intense delight of the listeners. And the songs of the Gael were sung, by a young man or a youthful

Smoking ruins along the River Liffey in Dublin following the Easter Rising, 1916.

*maiden, in that strain of passionate emotion which
only the language of the Gael can convey. This
indeed was the simple life of the country people, but
emigration was exacting a heavy toll, the young
men and women going by the tens of thousands.*

Due to the Famine and continuing emigration, the population of Killeagh parish declined
from 2,800 in 1841 to 900 in 1901. In the spring
of 1892, Tim Cashman joined the exodus, embarking from Queenstown on the Cunard liner
Catalonia, bound for Boston. Tim Cashman's
material baggage was pitifully small. But he
carried with him idyllic memories of his youth
and angry resentment of the poverty and oppression he held responsible for his exile.

THROUGHOUT THE 19TH century, the same
dream that animated Tim Cashman—the dream
of a free, prosperous, and beautiful Ireland—had
inspired others to action. The struggle that had
begun with Walter Devereux's United Irishmen
and the Wexford rebellion of 1798 had been
revived repeatedly over the decades.

In the 1820s the Irish Catholic lawyer and
orator Daniel O'Connell mobilized hundreds of
thousands of farmers and peasants behind his
crusade for "Catholic Emancipation." The movement successfully forced the repeal of the last
remaining Penal Laws that prevented Irish
Catholics from holding political office. Less
successfully, in the 1830s and early 1840s,

O'Connell also campaigned for the abolition of tithes to the Protestant church and for the restoration of Irish self-government.

In the mid-1840s, Richard O'Gorman and the Young Irelanders, led by William Smith O'Brien, repudiated O'Connell's peaceful form of agitation and launched their futile rebellion of 1848.

In the 1860s another former Young Ireland rebel, James Stephens, created the Irish Republican Brotherhood, better known as the Fenians, after Ireland's legendary pre-Christian warriors. With Irish American assistance, the Fenians staged their own rising against British rule in 1867. But it, too, was crushed.

Between 1879 and 1882 an unlikely combination of political leaders created the Irish Land League. Michael Davitt, son of a poor peasant from County Mayo, and Charles Stewart Parnell, a Cambridge-educated Protestant landlord, launched a "Land War" against Irish landlordism. On into the 20th century, Parnell and his successors mobilized Ireland's Catholics into the Home Rule movement, agitating for Irish self-government.

These repeated expressions of Irish nationalism in Ireland shaped the lives and hopes of millions of immigrants in America—immigrants such as Tim Cashman.

IN HIS MEMOIRS, Tim Cashman described America as "the 'Land of Liberty' so-called." Remembering his arrival in America in 1892, Cashman later wrote:

After some stormy weather, the shores of the new world hove in sight. The port of Boston was our disembarking place, and the wharf in East Boston where we landed was of a miserable, forbidding aspect. Dire poverty was to be seen all round, such wretched, horrible tenements with ragged, dirty, hungry-looking children playing in the ash-heaps of a nearby railroad. It created a bad impression on me on the spot. Thinks I to myself: "Is this the great country of 'peace and plenty' there is so much talk about?"

Tim Cashman went to Somerville, one of Boston's industrial suburbs, and found lodgings in an Irish American boardinghouse kept by a fellow Corkman. But even the company of fellow immigrants did not assuage Cashman's longing for the beauties of Glenbower Wood. The city's streets and factories were "too artificial," he wrote, "not like the green fields of my native land that I so dearly loved. How I missed mine own country at once!" His first work experiences were equally uncongenial. "I was given employment in a brass and copper foundry," he later recalled, "a hard, heavy job for a ten-hour day, with a tyrannical 'Boss' eternally forcing more work out of you if at all possible. It was a cruel, slavish species of employment, and I was a rebel against it from the first hour."

For several years, Tim Cashman searched for an employer who was not a "slave driver." He drifted from job to job, as a laborer in a soap factory and in a glass factory, as a dock-worker, and as a streetcar driver. At one point, Cashman took the civil service examination for employment in the Boston Customs House. He passed the test with a score of 98 out of 100. But when he learned he would have to pay a bribe to get the post he had earned fairly, he refused.

Timothy Cashman (1866–1934).

Instead, he took a job with the Boston Belting Company, a rubber manufactory in Roxbury, near Boston. Cashman's wages were "small" and he was "never satisfied, always looking for some better employment." Nevertheless, he would stay with the Boston Belting Company for more than 20 years because its officials "treated the employees fairly."

In 1902 Tim Cashman married an Irish immigrant, purchased a home in Roxbury, and began to raise a family. He also began to join a variety of Irish American societies and clubs.

Like his parents, Tim Cashman spoke Irish as well as English, and one of the organizations he joined was the Philo-Celtic Society devoted to the restoration of the ancient Irish language, which was fast disappearing even in his native parish. However, Tim Cashman was most devoted to his membership in another Irish American organization. This was the Clan na Gael, a secret revolutionary society headquartered in New York City whose leader, the elderly ex-Fenian John Devoy, tirelessly conspired for Irish independence. In Cashman's opinion, the leaders and members of the Clan na Gael were "the truest and staunchest friends of the Irish cause" in the United States. In fact, the Clan was only one of a long succession of Irish American nationalist organizations.

IN AMERICA, IRISH ETHNIC identity flourished on many fronts. Democratic politicians waved the green flag on election day and the Catholic clergy strove to preserve in America the religious aspects of Ireland's heritage. Irish American newspapers provided immigrant readers with news of the old country, giving the comforting impression that Boston or New York were merely western suburbs of Cork or Dublin. Above all, it was the Irish American ethnic organizations that helped immigrants like Tim Cashman become "reconciled to the American ways" and express their abiding love for Ireland and its "sacred cause."

Societies such as the Gaelic Athletic Association and the Philo-Celtic Society provided numerous continuities between Irish and Irish American life. But the most important of these societies, in symbolic terms, were the Irish American nationalist organizations.

Middle-class immigrants and many American-born Irish often joined because they hoped that the creation of a free and prosperous Ireland would help raise their own social status in the United States. Poor, working-class Irish immigrants and their children were usually the most devoted—even fanatical—adherents to Irish American nationalism.

Many of them were so alienated from a hostile American society and so inspired by hopes of "revenge for Skibbereen" that they planned to return home to fight for Irish freedom. Thomas Reilly, a homesick carpenter in upstate New York, wrote to a friend back in Dublin:

April 24, 1848
Dear John,

I am very sad, very lonely, very poor now indeed. Nothing save death could lull the storm which is raging in my mind. My young life is chequered enough, but it shall be, it must be more chequered.

There are Irish Volunteers preparing in America to invade Ireland in case of an emergency. My name is enrolled on the lists and we are drilling ourselves for the occasion.

Perhaps I will return to Ireland with the green flag flying above me. I care not if it becomes my shroud. I have no regard for life while I am in exile. We expect to muster 50,000 men in a short time. God send them soon. If that force were thrown on the southern coast of Ireland, we would quickly march to the city of Dublin and set it in a blaze.

So farewell, the dearest companion of my last years. I shall think of you in my hours of melancholy.

Thomas Reilly

One of the most important nationalist political movements in Ireland, the Fenians, also had a large and active division in the United States. In the 1860s, the American Fenians attracted millions of ardent sympathizers and raised a military force of 50,000 men, mostly veterans of the American Civil War. Their strategy was to return to Ireland to fight alongside their Irish comrades under the leadership of James Stephens. But American Fenian invasions of British Canada in 1866 and 1870 proved futile, and only a few hundred soldiers actually returned to Ireland to participate in the failed rebellion of 1867.

From the 1880s to 1916, many Irish immigrants and their children donated money to the cause of Home Rule for Ireland. The Irish Home Rule movement engaged in peaceful agitation, and its leaders demanded only a modest measure of Irish self-government. Most Irish Catholics at home and in the United States endorsed the Home Rule movement's goals and methods. But such pacific measures frustrated the more ardent revolutionaries in Ireland and America. Tim Cashman and his comrades in the Clan na Gael clung to the dream of total Irish independence and to the use of armed force to obtain it. "For the love of Ireland and the hate of England," begged one Irish American nationalist, "strike out, strike out strong."

By 1916 Tim Cashman had become a principal spokesman for Boston's branch of the Clan na Gael. "Let us hope," he prayed in one speech, "that before long we shall see a new Ireland, which shall be a nation." More quickly than even he might have imagined, Cashman's dreams began to come true.

A meeting of American Fenians, Philadelphia, Pennsylvania, 1865.

On April 24, 1916, the day after Easter Sunday, about 1,000 Irish rebels, mobilized by the Irish Republican Brotherhood and financed by the Clan na Gael, staged a revolution in Dublin. Led by Patrick Pearse, an idealistic schoolmaster, and James Connolly, a socialist labor leader, the rebels seized the General Post Office and other public buildings in the center of the city and proclaimed the creation of an Irish republic. By the time they surrendered, one week later, downtown Dublin was devastated by British artillery and more than 400 rebels, Irish civilians, and British soldiers had been killed.

At first, the rebels did not have wide support among the Irish people at home or abroad. But the executions of Pearse, Connolly, and the other leaders of the Easter Rising by British firing squads galvanized Irish and Irish American anger against the British government.

Over the next two years, the old Home Rule movement disintegrated, replaced by a much more militant political party. Its name, Sinn Féin, meant "Ourselves Alone" and signified its leaders' goal of total Irish independence. In the British election of December 1918, Sinn Féin won nearly every parliamentary seat in Ireland's Catholic constituencies. But the Sinn Féin representatives refused to take their seats in the British Parliament. In January 1919 they met in Dublin and declared their assembly to be the government of a free Irish Republic. At the same time, military leader Michael Collins was welding the remnants of the Easter rebels and fresh recruits into a new and more deadly fighting force—the Irish Republican Army (IRA). From 1919 until late June 1921, the IRA fought a fierce guerilla war against British forces in Ireland.

In June 1919, when the War for Irish Independence was just beginning, Eamon de Valera, the president of the Irish Republic's shadow government, came to the United States seeking financial and political support for an independent Ireland. U.S. President Woodrow Wilson had claimed that the American government fought World War I to liberate small nations from their imperial masters. But neither his Democratic administration nor the Republican Party leadership was willing to pressure Great Britain on Ireland's behalf.

Irish Americans, however, welcomed de Valera, supported his cause with enormous enthusiasm, and contributed over $10 million to the Irish Republic. That financial support enabled Collins and the IRA to wage their War for Independence. Eventually they forced the British government to the bargaining table, and in De-

Dead "Sinn Féiners" in the streets, 1920.

cember 1921, a treaty was negotiated establishing the Irish Free State.

Because Michael Collins and the Irish Republican Army had been unable to defeat the British totally, the treaty that Collins negotiated with the British represented only a partial victory. Some of Collins' comrades were dissatisfied, and in 1922–23 the new nation was plunged into civil war. Moreover, the treaty partitioned the island. Above a new border, six Ulster counties were named "Northern Ireland" and remained part of Great Britain. With a Protestant majority but a large, unhappy Catholic minority, Northern Ireland was destined to be a continued source of political strife and, after 1968, violent conflict.

Still, after centuries of struggle against British rule, most of Ireland was free. On March 17, 1922, Denis Hurley of Carson City, Nevada—like Tim Cashman a transplanted Corkman—wrote jubilantly to his brother in Ireland:

My dear John,

We all feel much better over the improved state of affairs in Ireland. The cleaning out of Dublin Castle was a great change. Now we all can sing the "Wearing of the Green" on the anniversary of our Patron Saint. I hope the people will make good use of the liberties they have won and make the land contented and prosperous.

Regards to all,
Denis

Irish American nationalists were fortunate that their dollars and devotion had helped to liberate Ireland by 1921. In retrospect, it appears that they were fighting a losing battle, not only against the might of the British Empire, but also against the inexorable forces of time. Nearly all the old Irish immigrants who remembered the Famine had died, and the number of new immigrants were dwindling. Most Irish Americans had been born in America, not Ireland. They were increasingly prosperous and content, and less prone to regard themselves as exiles seeking vengeance for old wrongs.

However, old men like John Devoy and new recruits such as Tim Cashman had kept the Fenian flame alive, burning in the hearts of the immigrants' children and grandchildren. "We have fought the good fight," rejoiced one Irish American. "We have kept the faith. We have loved our God and dear old Ireland." The long winter of Irish exile in America seemed finally over.

Irish American women demanding President Woodrow Wilson's support for Irish freedom from Great Britain, 1920.

CHAPTER TEN

MIRACULOUS ENERGY

IN 1857 RICHARD O'GORMAN had written that Irish immigrants were "imbued with miraculous energy" when they touched American soil. Certainly, by the early 20th century Irish American energies seemed to be coursing through every vein of American society.

> Now the Kellys run the statehouse,
> And the Kellys run the banks,
> The police and fire departments,
> Sure the Kellys fill the ranks.
> Dan Kelly runs the railroads,
> John Kelly runs the seas,
> Kate Kelly runs the suffragettes
> And she looks right good to me.
> Well I went and asked directions
> From a naturalized Chinese,
> But he said, "Please excuse me but
> My name it is Kell Lee."
> And there's Kelly from Dublin,
> Kelly from Sligo,
> Little Mickey Kelly
> Who came from the County Clare.
> Sure Kelly built the pyramids
> With good old Galway granite,
> And when Kelly discovered the North Pole,
> Sure he found Pat Kelly there.

The McGoverns, immigrants from County Cavan, and their children, Philadelphia, Pennsylvania, 1904.

Over the course of the 20th century the number of Irish-born in America has been dwarfed by the much larger immigrations of people from Southern and Eastern Europe, Latin America, the Caribbean, and Asia. But during the early decades of this century, when the economic, social, and cultural foundations of contemporary America were established, it did indeed appear that, in O'Gorman's words, "something Irish is prominent everywhere."

By the early 1900s the Irish had achieved remarkable economic success, reaching approximately the same occupational levels as other Americans. Among Irish American men, for example, 35 percent held white-collar jobs, 50 percent were skilled workers, and only 15 percent remained unskilled laborers. Moreover, the educational attainment of Irish American Catholics, measured by the number of school years completed, actually exceeded that of native-born white Protestants.

Of course, by 1900 the overwhelming majority of Irish Americans had been born in the United States, and their accomplishments generally far surpassed those of their immigrant parents. In Boston the American-born Irish were four times more likely to hold white-collar positions than were their immigrant parents. And they were much more likely to live in the new suburbs that were beginning to spread beyond the old working-class neighborhoods.

Irish power in the Democratic Party, in city and state governments, in the nation's largest labor unions, and in the Catholic Church had

Irish entrepreneurs
in South Boston, Massa-
chusetts, 1916.

laid the foundations for these economic achieve-
ments. And in turn, by the 1920s this economic
success had provided stepping stones for Irish
American penetration—indeed, for Irish American leadership—in all aspects of American life.
In the 1920s, Al Smith, William Green, and
Cardinal James Gibbons were the most powerful
figures in the Democratic Party, the American
Federation of Labor, and the Catholic Church,
respectively. Other sons and grandsons of Irish
immigrants, such as John McGraw, George M.
Cohan, Eugene O'Neill, and F. Scott Fitzgerald,
dominated American baseball, music, theatre,
and literature.

In the 1920s the Kellys, and a thousand
other Irish names, seemed to be everywhere and,
as O'Gorman had written, they were there for evil
as well as good. Irish Americans such as "Bugs"
Moran and "Legs" Diamond were still prominent
figures in the nation's underworld!

"AMERICA IS CHANGE," historian Dennis
Clark has asserted, "and immigration is one of
the great modern dramas of change. So in order
to understand the novelty of America, the im-
pulse and momentum that have made America a
society of change, we must understand that the
people who came here were ready for change.
Hence, immigration almost prefigures the way
that Americans look at society."

Despite their nostalgia for Ireland, Irish
immigrants would not have fared so well in
America had they not adapted so successfully to
a society that was far more fluid and dynamic
than the Irish villages they had abandoned. And
the decade of the 1920s was perhaps the most
fluid and dynamic of all, as new automobiles,
radios, cinema, music, and slang reshaped American culture in dramatically nontraditional ways.
Older Irish Americans often found the transition
between Irish family values and the new cults of
youth and beauty profoundly unsettling. However, few Irish immigrants adapted more thor-
oughly to F. Scott Fitzgerald's "Jazz Age" than
James Quinn, alias Tim O'Brien.

THE 18-YEAR-OLD SON of a Catholic police-man, James Quinn lived in Belfast, on the Upper Falls Road. Deeply devoted to his mother, but in conflict with his hard-drinking and abusive father, Quinn ran away from home in 1920 and emigrated to America to seek and find adventures such as few Irish immigrants ever imagined.

Perhaps because he entered the United States illegally—by hijacking at gunpoint a train crossing the U.S.-Canadian border!—Quinn changed his name to Tim O'Brien. Under that alias he sent a steady stream of postcards and short letters home to his mother in Belfast, expressing his boyish delight at the wonders of modern American life.

January 1921
Dear Mother,

Here I am in New York City. No-one here shines his own shoes, but has it done every day for ten cents in a shine parlor. We eat in automatic cafes—put in a nickel or a dime and pull out your favorite dinner from a machine, or sit on a high stool at a lunch counter and have a "hash slinger" shoot it to you. Am starting for South America tomorrow.

Love,
Tim

Tim O'Brien not only went to South America, down the west coast from Panama to Ecuador; he crossed the entire continent, alone and on foot through the Amazon jungles, and wrote his next letter from the east coast of Brazil!

November 1921

Well, sir, this kid thought he knew something before he left Guayaquil, Ecuador, for Pará, Brazil, about 4,000 miles across a continent, but it was an experience known only to a few. Travelled with the "Jivaro" head-hunters unharmed. Someday I'll write out the whole works and put it in a magazine.

From Brazil, Tim O'Brien sailed to New Orleans, where he was celebrated as the "boy explorer." Lionized by the press, O'Brien gained a thirst for notoriety that drove him across the United States in a tireless search for new exploits and everlasting fame.

December 1921. On board train, Mississippi.
Dear Mother,

There was no difficulty for yours truly when it came to getting ashore sans passport with my curios from the head-hunter country. This morning I left New Orleans, my fare paid for by the Museum people to whom I have loaned my Indian collections. The newspapers tell me I can easily clear $500 on the first story and a few thousand after that in the book form. You're going to have a son you can be proud of, Mammy.

James Quinn, aka Tim O'Brien (1902–1924).

After leaving New Orleans, Tim O'Brien tried to become a writer in New York's Greenwich Village, a rodeo cowboy in Texas, and a newspaper correspondent in Mexico. None of these careers brought him the success or the celebrity he craved. But O'Brien's energy was irrepressible, and by late 1922 he was ready for another adventure. He headed for Hollywood, California, the "American Babylon" and capital of the nation's movie industry in which, O'Brien was sure, he would soon become a star.

Broadway between 3rd and 4th, Los Angeles, California, 1920s.

October 1922

Los Angeles is a wild place, Mammy. Hold'ups and murders are more numerous here than in any town in the Union. But I can't kick. I like a town full of life, and I'm hitting on all six. I've got a new "sweet mama." She shakes shimmy on "Cleopatra" scenes over at Ingraham's studios. A perfect blonde! Hot dogs!!

Tim O'Brien never attained cinematic stardom. In his letters he boasted of his acquaintance with Charlie Chaplin and Douglas Fairbanks, but at best he was an "extra" and a stunt man in some of Tom Mix's silent westerns. However, he loved the pace and glitter of Los Angeles. And at first he did make money, enough to purchase plenty of "bootleg" liquor and a used Buick sedan to impress his "sweet mamas" and his dissolute friends. His earnings came not from the movies, but from selling religious statues to Catholic migrants from Mexico!

May 1923

God, I never knew I was alive 'til I got out here and woke up. Money is a wonderful key to happiness. California is going to be my home, mama, and I wish you could decide to come out and live with me. At present I'm doing well selling, but I lack capital. Do you know anyone who wants in on the ground floor of a 20,000 barrel a day proposition? No, it's not oil, it's Virgins. The Blessed Mother sells better than popcorn to the Latin element in California.

By the spring of 1924 Tim O'Brien's careers as an author, journalist, movie actor, salesman—even as a professional boxer—had failed, and he was forced to fall back on his tarnished reputation as the boy explorer. He exhibited his curios and retold his Amazon experiences for 25 cents a customer on the boardwalk at Long Beach. As far as one could tell from his letters home, though, fame and fortune were still just around the corner.

April 6, 1924
Dearest Mother,

My curios—shrunken heads, etc.—have been released from the L.A. Museum and I have started my own road show. We had our World Premiere some time ago and left Los Angeles to tour the U.S. Maybe we'll go as far as your country. For now, I got to beat it around to the dump, get my megaphone, and startle creation with my "Head Shrinkers of the Amazon." There's a line of guys at two-bits apiece waiting to see "Captain O'Brien," the explorer, so I'll say "Adios."

Tim

Tim O'Brien's story about the origin of the curios he was exhibiting was apparently false. On May 20, 1924, two Los Angeles police detectives, Lieutenants Bartley and Shammo, pricked up their ears when they heard a barker at the Long Beach pike inviting spectators to see "the only shrunken human heads in captivity." Several months earlier, a valuable collection of shrunken heads and other Amazonian artifacts had been stolen from a Los Angeles anthropologist. The detectives arrested Tim O'Brien, and on August 5, 1924, he was found guilty of first-degree burglary. However, the judge agreed that O'Brien was eligible to be released on bail, pending his appeal of the sentence. That was a big mistake, for

"Captain O'Brien" was nothing if not resourceful and elusive.

September 22, 1924
Havana, Cuba
Darling Mother,

Just taking a trip east to New York on the "Venezuela" for a rest. We have been three weeks afloat, calling at many Central American ports. With the help of God and the White Star line, we'll soon be together again.

Love,
Tim

Tim O'Brien never told his mother the true story of his arrest, conviction, and escape from the clutches of the law. That brief letter was the last she ever heard of him. He never returned to his Belfast home, and no record of him appears in either Havana or New York City. Tim O'Brien seems to have vanished without a trace.

The passenger vessel *Venezuela*, 1920s.

IN THE DECADES AFTER World War II, it appeared to some observers that a distinct Irish America had vanished, like Tim O'Brien, into the anonymous mass of America's population. The number of new Irish immigrants steadily dwindled from the 1920s through the 1960s, and so Irish America was increasingly composed of those who had few or no memories of Ireland or even of their ancestors' immigrant experience. The election of John F. Kennedy in 1960 apparently marked the final adaptation and acceptance of the Irish in the United States. And in the decades since, most of the 40 million Americans who claim Irish descent seem largely indistinguishable from their suburban neighbors.

Many of the old indices of Irishness have blurred or even disappeared in the American melting pot. As they moved into the upper echelons of the nation's corporations and country clubs, Irish Americans often abandoned the Democratic Party for Eisenhower or Reagan Republicanism. Tammany Hall, last run by Italian rather than Irish Americans, is only a relic of the past, and nearly all the old Irish political machines have disintegrated or been taken over by other groups. The Irish no longer dominate the American labor movement. Many Irish Americans have become little more than nominal Catholics in the more secular atmosphere of the past few decades.

Even for Americans born in Ireland, it became increasingly difficult to preserve and transmit a sense of Irish identity to their children and grandchildren. Or so lamented Mary Dunleavy, an elderly immigrant from County Roscommon, to her nephew in Ireland:

July 15, 1966
My dear nephew,

From my long delay in answering your letter, I hope you will not get the impression that I did not appreciate your extensive historical research on our family in Ireland and the conditions that brought about our emigration. I truly did. But I am sorry to say that the younger generation here have shown very little interest in the history of their forebears.

I couldn't explain to you the attitude of the people born here. This is their country, and what went before is no concern of theirs. We have had to fight to keep even a vestige of their Irish background alive. All they worry about is education, making money, and having a good time.

Lovingly,
Your Aunt Mary

Mary Dunleavy's disappointment was understandable, for the normal gaps between older and younger generations were widened even further by the distance between the old country and the new. Still, it is difficult to be too critical of the children and grandchildren of immigrants for seeking material comforts and personal fulfillment. After all, those were precisely the ambi-

(Facing) St. Patrick's Day Paraders, marching proudly past St. Patrick's Cathedral, New York City. (Below) The McGoverns, the children of immigrants from County Cavan, enjoying their success in America, 1928.

In memory of
PATRICK FLANAGAN
BORN
COUNTY ROSCOMMON
IRELAND
DEC. 25, 1817
DIED
DEC. 31, 1892
REQUIESCAT IN PACE

FLANAGAN

The grave of Patrick Flanagan, who was born in County Roscommon on December 25, 1817, and died in Junction City, Kansas, on December 31, 1892.

tions that brought their ancestors out of Ireland to the United States.

Moreover, in the decade after Mary Dunleavy wrote her letter, the attitudes of the younger generation began to change. Irish Americans, young and old, began to rediscover and celebrate their Irish identity. In recent years many have embraced the proposition of American-born dramatist Eugene O'Neill that "Nothing says more about me than the fact that I am Irish."

In part, the upsurge of Irish American consciousness is a reflection of concern over the contemporary violence in Northern Ireland. Also, new waves of Irish immigrants, many of them

illegal, have revived once-moribund Irish neighborhoods in New York, Boston, and other American cities. More broadly, it is a reflection of the pervasive "Roots" phenomenon—a longing for identification and meaning amidst the increasing impersonality and uncertainty of modern American society.

Whatever its causes, the result has been what Dennis Clark calls "a tremendous cultural revival." In cities throughout the United States, Irish American social clubs, centers for historical research, classes in traditional Irish music, dancing, and even the Irish language have emerged

grants are flocking to American shores, perhaps one can learn necessary and valuable lessons from the stories of those who preceded them to the New World. Historian Hasia Diner has reflected: "If we can come to an understanding of one group that was compelled to leave its homeland, to transplant itself someplace new, to pick and choose among the options the New World had to offer them, to pick and choose among the sort of baggage they brought and to create a new culture, a new response to a new environment, then we have gone a long way, not only towards understanding American society, but towards understanding a very fundamental human experience."

"It is impossible to understand people," Dennis Clark argues, "unless we understand their origins, unless we understand the flagrant and subtle ways in which childhood affects all of us. The imprint of Ireland made the Irish immigrants what they were, and when they brought that to America it not only made them behave and think in certain ways, but they passed on parts of that imprint to their children, their grandchildren, even to their great-grandchildren."

In a sense, the Irish American revival is an attempt to identify that Irish imprint. Some search for it in traditional Irish songs, music, and dances. Others read books or take extension courses in Irish and Irish American history. And many others trace their geneology, piecing together from family bibles and fading memories the story of their family in America. For them, the great prize is to identify their immigrant ancestors—the men and women who first came out of Ireland, with hope and joy, anger and trepidation, to create a new life in America.

and flourished. Irish America's "miraculous energy" has not died, after all.

Sometimes it appears that nearly all Americans, not just those of Irish background, have embraced Ireland's heritage. Irish Americans such as William Kennedy and Mary Gordon are best-selling novelists. Irish movies such as *My Left Foot* and *In the Name of the Father* have been box-office as well as artistic successes. And Irish musicians from U2 to Sinead O'Connor dominate the world's pop charts.

Some critics regard the revived interest in Irish American ethnicity as insular and divisive. However, at a time when millions of new immi-

CHAPTER ELEVEN

ERIN ONCE MORE

Oh! when will the exile return?
Oh! when will the exile return?
When our hearts heave no sigh,
When our tears shall be dry,
When Erin no longer shall mourn …
Oh! then will the exile return.

On both sides of the Atlantic Ocean, the folklore of Irish Catholic emigration is dominated by the image of the homesick emigrant as exile. Yet, one of the great ironies of Irish history is that so few Irish immigrants to the United States actually did return, either to visit or to remain permanently in the land of their birth.

Among Italian immigrants to America, more than 40 percent returned to live in their homeland. Among Poles and Hungarians, more than 50 percent returned. And among Greek immigrants, more than 60 percent went back to their native land. But fewer than 10 percent of Irish immigrants to the New World ever returned to "Mother Ireland."

One Irish immigrant who did return was Tim Cashman, the Boston laborer and Irish American nationalist whose loving memories of Glenbower Wood inspired his longing for home. However, the story of Cashman's return to Ireland sadly illustrates why so few Irish immigrants have followed his example.

IN 1925, IN THE WAKE of the successful Irish struggle for freedom, Tim Cashman retired from his job in Roxbury and bought passage on a steamship back to Ireland. His ship's destination was the same Irish seaport from which he had embarked for Boston 33 years earlier. In the 19th century the British government had named the port "Queenstown," after Queen Victoria. Now, however, the town had been rechristened with its ancient Irish name of "Cobh" by the newly independent government of the Irish Free State.

From the beginning of his voyage, Cashman kept a journal, hoping to record his joyful reunion with the scenes of his youth:

Sunday, July 19, 1925. Here I am on board the steamship "Laconia" from Boston bound for Cobh, Ireland, after months of hesitation. After thirty-three years I am gladdened at this moment more than I can express in words or writing, with the thought of seeing dear old Erin once more.

Wednesday, July 29, 1925. We arrived at Cobh at last. I put my foot on shore at the customs house in the morning at four A.M. My heart sank as I saw the street at that early hour without a soul abroad, and in looking out at the harbor overhung with dark lowering clouds, it presented a scene of desolation. You'd imagine the houses were built before Abraham's time, ancient looking, everything without life.

I got to Killeagh before eleven o'clock and 'twas rainy and cold. Mud and dirt all over everything.

The Vale of Avoca, County Wicklow.

Walking over the mud-covered little street, everything looked so curious to me, familiar, yet not familiar. I can't get my eyes to see things as they were to me before I left.

I have visited the remains of my old home. Standing there on the floor, which is now grass-grown, what memories came to me. I stood there in sad contemplation, thinking of the times when the family lived together, father, mother, sister and brothers. The tears came to my eyes. Cattle grazing around and looking curiously towards me as if they'd ask the question, "What are you doing here?"

Timothy Cashman as an older man.

As an ardent nationalist, Cashman was disappointed that the Anglo-Irish Treaty of 1921 had partitioned the island, leaving northern Ireland still part of Great Britain. However, he was far more distressed that in southern Ireland, Irish poverty and emigration seemed as great in 1925 as when he had left his home in 1892. The parish of Killeagh now had merely 700 inhabitants, 300 fewer than when he had emigrated. In 1925 alone, nearly 40,000 Irish men and women left the island to seek their fortunes overseas.

Patrick Pearse, one of the leaders of the Easter Rebellion of 1916, had dreamed that "a free Ireland would not, and could not, have hunger in her fertile vales and squalor in her cities." However, his fellow rebel, the socialist James Connolly, had wisely predicted that winning political independence alone would neither ensure Irish economic prosperity nor stop Irish emigration. More radical measures, he argued, would be necessary.

The conservative leaders of independent Ireland never adopted Connolly's sweeping reforms. Emigration continued to the United States in the 1920s, and at even higher levels to Britain in the 1940s and 1950s. In the 1960s and 1970s Ireland's economy expanded significantly and emigration abated. But in the 1980s the Irish "economic miracle" came at least to a temporary halt. New waves of Irish immigrated, many of them illegally, into the United States. Today, despite the promises of past nationalists and contemporary politicians, Ireland's most valuable export continues to be her own people.

IN MANY RESPECTS, THE STORY of Ireland's immigrants is the story of all humanity in the modern world. Society changes so rapidly that it is increasingly difficult to deal with the reality of change using the ideas, concepts, and rhetoric of the past. And so, like the Irish, we find ourselves in a sort of exile.

What the immigrants experienced in moving from the Irish countryside to American cities is not that dissimilar from the experience so many of us still have today: constantly uprooted, constantly searching for a better job or a better house—whether in a newer suburb still farther out of town or in a newer city with a more dynamic economy. Yet, like the Irish immigrants, most of us still yearn nostalgically for some sort of fancied security—some timeless sense of place and meaning and belonging—that we had, or imagine we had, as children. And so, to paraphrase F. Scott Fitzgerald, we run faster and faster, hoping some day to catch up with a past which we have irretrievably lost.

SUNSET OFF HOWTH. 658. W.L.

Sunset off Howth,
County Dublin.

Most Irish immigrants did not try to go "home." Instead of enduring the pain of return, they comforted themselves with a harmless, if sometimes trivialized, nostalgia for the "Old Sod." Perhaps they understood something that Tim Cashman did not.

For while Cashman's recollections of Ireland were frozen at the moment of his departure, time had transformed both the land and the people almost beyond recognition. On the one hand, Ireland seemed stagnant and impoverished compared with America. On the other hand, everything he had cherished in his memories had, in the words of Irish poet W. B. Yeats, "changed, changed utterly." Indeed, he had become an exile in the very land of his birth.

Timothy Cashman spent only a few weeks in Ireland revisiting the haunts of his youth. Before he left, he walked again in Glenbower Wood, the place that was, for him, the embodiment of Mother Ireland. There, in the stone of an old bridge, he carved his name in Gaelic script. Then he left and came home … home to America.

CREDITS

LETTER AND MEMOIR SOURCES: **Maurice Woulfe**: C. O. Danachair, Dublin; **Walter Devereux**: Devereux Papers, Friedsam Library Archives, St. Bonaventure University; John Devereux Kernan; **Mary Rush**: *British Parliamentary Papers*, 1847; Claude Bourguignon; **Daniel Guiney**: Irish National Archives; **William Dever**: Miss M. A. Timoney; **William Murphy**: Deputy Keeper, Public Record Office Of Northern Ireland (PRONI); **T. McIntyre**: Deputy Keeper, Public Record Office Of Northern Ireland (PRONI); **Patrick Walsh**: Cork Examiner, National Library of Ireland; **James Dixon**: Arnold Schrier Collection; **Patrick Dunny**: Arnold Schrier Collection; **Richard O'Gorman**: Smith O'Brien Papers, National Library of Ireland; **Margaret M'Carthy**: Irish National Archives; **Alexander Sproule**: A. J. Sproule Papers, Southern Historical Collection, University of North Carolina–Chapel Hill; **Mary Brown**: Arnold Schrier Collection; **Mary Ann Rowe**: Mrs. Brid Galway; **Tom Brick**: Kevin and James Brick; **W. H. Downes**: Mrs. Delia McNamara; **Arthur Quin**: Deputy Keeper, Public Record Office Of Northern Ireland (PRONI); **Thomas Reilly**: National Library of Ireland; **Denis Hurley**: Cork Archives Institute; **James Quinn/Tim O'Brien**: Maeve Cregan, Francis Keating, Marie Gribben; **Mary Dunleavy**: Anonymous donor; **Timothy Cashman**: Patrick Clancy, Timothy Cashman.

PHOTOGRAPHY AND ILLUSTRATION SOURCES: **1**: Hogg Collection, Ulster Museum; **2-3**: Lawrence Collection, National Library of Ireland; **4**: Langham Collection, Ulster Museum; **7**: Department of Folklore, University College Dublin; **9**: Culver Pictures; **10**: Lawrence Collection, National Library of Ireland; **11**: National Park Service, Ellis Island Immigration Museum; **12**: Lawrence Collection, National Library of Ireland; **13**: The John F. Kennedy Library; **14**: Society for the Preservation of New England Antiquities; **15**: Lawrence Collection, National Library of Ireland; **16**: Welch Collection, Ulster Museum; **18**: Bellamont Forest Album, National Library of Ireland; **19**: Lawrence Collection, National Library of Ireland; **20**: Oneida County Historical Society; **21 (both)**: *History of the Irish Rebellion in 1798*; **22-23 (upper)**: Library of Congress; **23 (lower right)**: John Devereux Kernan; **24**: Lawrence Collection, National Library of Ireland; **25**: *Illustrated London News*; **26**: *Illustrated London News*; **27**: Lawrence Collection, National Library of Ireland; **28**: National Library of Ireland; **30**: *Harper's Weekly*; **31**: *Harper's Weekly*; **33**: Lawrence Collection, National Library of Ireland; **34**: M. Patrick Roach; **35**: M. Patrick Roach; **36**: Society for the Preservation of New England Antiquities; **38**: Beaver Island Historical Society; **39**: Immigrant City Archives; **40**: Library of Congress; **41**: Library of Congress; **42**: Welch Collection, Ulster Museum; **43**: Idaho Historical Society; **44**: Library of Congress; **45**: A. J. Russell Collection, The Oakland Museum History Department; **46**: G. E. Anderson Collection, Harold B. Lee Library, Brigman Young University; **47**: Records of the Forest Service, National Archives:; **48**: Bethlehem Steel Corporation Collection, Hugh Moore Historical Parks and Museums; **49**: Snyder Collection, University of Missouri-Kansas City Libraries; **50**: New-York Historical Society, NYC; **51**: Library of Congress; **52**: New York Public Library; **53**: Erie Canal Museum; **54**: *Harper's Weekly*; **55**: Print Department, Boston Public Library; **56**: Lester S. Levy Collection, Milton S. Eisenhower Library, The Johns Hopkins University; **57**: Society for the Preservation of New England Antiquities; **59**: The Archives of Labor and Urban Affairs, Wayne State University; **60**: Lawrence Collection, National Library of Ireland; **61**: Library of Congress; **62-63 (upper)**: New-York Historical Society, NYC; **63 (lower)**: *Harper's Weekly*; **64**: The Bostonian Society/Old State House; **65**: Howard Applegate Collection, The Balch Institute for Ethnic Studies Library; **66**: William D. Griffin; **68**: Library of Congress; **71**: National Park Service, Ellis Island Immigration Museum; **72**: Lawrence Collection, National Library of Ireland; **73**: Ulster Folk and Transport Museum; **74**: Welch Collection, Ulster Museum; **75**: Department of Folklore, University College Dublin; **76**: Walsh Family; **77**: Dedham Historical Society; **78**: Alice Austen Collection, Staten Island Historical Society; **79**: Watchorn Memorial Methodist Church; **80**: Library of Congress; **81**: Alice Austen Collection, Staten Island Historical Society; **82**: Lawrence Collection, National Library of Ireland; **83**: Alice Austen Collection, Staten Island Historical Society; **84**: Lawrence Collection, National Library of Ireland; **85**: Kevin Brick; **86**: Lawrence Collection, National Library of Ireland; **87**: Lawrence Collection, National Library of Ireland; **88**: The South Dakota State Historical Society; **89**: Kevin Brick; **90**: Charles F. Taylor; **91**: Beaver Island Historical Society; **92**: Immigrant City Archives; **93**: Minnesota Historical Society; **95**: Frank Clark Collection, University of Notre Dame; **96**: Immigrant City Archives; **97**: Beaver Island Historical Society; **98**: Catholic University Archives; **99**: Library of Congress; **100**: Department of Folklore, University College Dublin; **101**: Hogg Collection, Ulster Museum; **102**: Father Edward Ryan Stewart; **103**: Archives, Archdiocese of Boston; **104**: Knights of Columbus Supreme Council Photo Archives; **105**: Archives, Archdiocese of Boston; **106**: Hulton Deutsch Collection; **108**: Valentine Collection, National Library of Ireland; **109**: Timothy Cashman; **111**: *Harper's Weekly*; **112**: Hulton Deutsch Collection; **113**: Library of Congress; **115**: McGovern Family Photographs, The Balch Institute for Ethnic Studies Library; **116**: Society for the Preservation of New England Antiquities; **117**: Francis Keating; **118**: California Historical Society, Title Insurance and Trust Photo Collection, Department of Special Collections, University of Southern California Library; **119**: San Francisco Chronicle Collection, San Francisco Maritime National Historical Park; **120**: The Bettmann Archive; **121**: McGovern Family Photographs, The Balch Institute for Ethnic Studies Library; **122-123**: Joseph J. Pennell Collection, Kansas Collection, University of Kansas Libraries; **124**: Lawrence Collection, National Library of Ireland; **126**: Timothy Cashman; **127**: Lawrence Collection, National Library of Ireland; **128**: Department of Folklore, University College Dublin.

A woman of the windswept Aran Islands, just off the west coast of Ireland.

INDEX